Life of a Cockney

From UK to Canada to USA

Robert Edward Scanes

Paperback: 979-8-218-17053-0
First paperback edition 2023

Library of Congress Control Number: 2023904258

Edited and Cover Design by Carole R. Scanes
Book Design by Madeline Sweeney
Printed in the USA by Village Books
Chloe Hovind and Jessica Moreland, Publishing Team, Village
Books

*This book is a memoir. It reflects the author's memories of events
and locations in his life. As his daughter, I have made every effort to
correct spelling and verify locations.*

"Memory... is the diary we all carry about with us"
                                                -Oscar Wilde

Life of a Cockney
From UK to Canada to USA

Daughter's Foreword

My father, Robert Edward Scanes was described in various reference letters as methodical, honest, efficient, pernicious (swift and nimble), reliable, intelligent, and hardworking. These characteristics are all evident in his autobiography.

I am Rob's (as his mum called him) oldest daughter, Carole Scanes. I have edited, included photos, and added a final word. Robert's life was so varied and encompassed a wide range of geography and experiences. Starting in the UK to his 6-year service in the Royal Air Force in England, during WWII to immigrating to Canada then the United States to pursue his career in the aircraft industry as well as to find a better life and opportunities for his growing family.

Bob was always creating, repairing, building and challenging himself with new interests. He was a great learner and teacher of his many passions. He loved to draw, dance, paint, wood work, travel, hike, ski, socialize and make soup!

I loved and admired my father deeply. Often I find myself realizing how much like him I can be. I know he would be so appreciative to have his life story published and that has kept me moving forward with this project.

I hope you will enjoy reading his varied and extraordinary life adventures, written in his own words.

Robert Edward Scanes, Wittering, England 1954

Chapter 1

THE EARLY YEARS

Robert Edward Scanes
Born April 21, 1924

A true Englishman, I was born in London on April 21, 1925, within the sound of Bow Bells, on the same day of the month as the Queen of England, but one year before. To be born within the sound of Bow qualifies a person to be called a Cockney. Buckingham Palace is also within the sound of Bow, so Prince Charles is a good, true Cockney. My address was 14 Emmett St. Poplar, in the East End of London. I said the address *was*, because this area was one of the most bombed areas in the city, and it was more or less completely destroyed during WW11.

My grandmother was eighty-two the last time I saw her. She stayed in London throughout the German's blitz, and survived. I never saw my grandfather. He died in 1930 at the age of seventy. My father and I used to visit my grandmother occasionally. We would catch an early steam train from Addlestone, 20 miles south west of the city to Waterloo. We left the station via Waterloo Road, a cobble street, and rode on one of the old open trams. People on the tram's top deck had to sit in the rain with a piece of canvas affixed to the back of the seat in front to pull over their lap. The seats in those days were wooden slats with no padding. Most of the buses and trams had open tops. I don't remember ever going when it was not raining. We would get off the tram at Greenwich and walk to the elevator to go down to the level of the Greenwich pedestrian tunnel. The tunnel was under the Thames River, at least half a mile long, made for walking only. It was completely lined with white tile. It was always interesting to me at that age to be walking under the water. Our next ride was by bus to Mill Wall.

I remember very well the last time I saw my grandmother. She took us to the end of her garden and showed us her little Anderson bomb shelter, where they slept during air raids. My father's sister, Lilly, lived near her by the docks. She also stayed there throughout the war. It was amazing what they endured. The docks were the most heavily bombed areas in the city. Nearly everything we needed to survive, came to us by sea.

My father, Richard Scanes, was born and raised in the East End of London. He had five brothers and a sister. I have no details of his youth until after he left school when he served an apprenticeship as a wood machinist. Early in the First World War, he joined the Royal Navy as a cook and served on a number of His Majesty's ships in various parts of the world. It was while he was in the service that he and my mother met and were later married in 1923.

My mother, Emily Margaret Bates, was born and raised in a little village called Old Byfleet in the county of Surrey about twenty miles south west of London. She had two sisters and a brother; Lena, Jess, and Ted. My mother was the youngest and was born with a problem with her right leg. She had to go through numerous operations as a child to correct it. I never had any details, but I know she had a weakness and a problem that was with her all of her life.

My uncle Ted immigrated to Canada in the twenties. He owned a butcher shop in Rosetown, Saskatchewan. He was married to Rose and they had a son, also named Ted. The son was killed in an automobile accident. Later, after my uncle Ted died, Rose returned to England, but I never did meet her.

My Uncle Bill was regional manager for the East London Electric Company. They had three boys Bill, Harry and Reg. All three boys were in the service, and all three survived the war, which given the odds was amazing.

Three years after I was born in 1928, the year of the general strike and the beginning of the depression, my parents decided that it would be good to move to Old Byfleet to get away from the fog and general city environment. They were trying to improve their lives and take me to a healthier area. With the declining economy, there was very little or no work in Byfleet, or anywhere else, so they started a retail fish business in partnership with my mother's stepfather Jack Hollick. For the move to Old Byfleet, they were able to use the horse and cart that was purchased to begin the business. I can just picture them with the cart full of furniture going for twenty plus miles with one of them having to walk.

The business started off well. There was a need for a fresh fish delivery in the area. My father would get up at two in the morning and travel to Billings Gate Fish Market to buy the fresh fish. He would arrive back in Old Byfleet around 7:00 A.M. so that he and his partner could make their rounds selling the fish. It was tough at first, but things were off to a good start and the demand began to increase. It was a success until his partner began drinking during the day. This happened when my father went to rest preparing for the next morning.

It wasn't long before there were problems with the fish spoiling and people were getting dissatisfied with unreliable deliveries. Shortly after the drinking started the business failed. It was a great disappointment, but there was nothing anyone could do but to give it up and find other work.

Robert, often called Rob or Bob
1932

Visiting my grandmother in East London

Sadly, during the depth of the depression, there was no work to be had. Things were hard for my parents. Keeping food on the table and paying the rent was difficult.

It was fortunate that they were able to rent a small house owned by Aunt Nell and Uncle Stan. At least we had a roof over our heads. Aunt Nell must have been my mother's aunt. It was a small, two-room building with a partition separating the rooms. I can remember lying in bed listening to them talk in the other room.

Another person, who wasn't really a relation, but who had a big influence in my life, was a lady I used to call Aunt Dick. She was in those days considered a spinster and was a sister to the church at Lambeth, a sort of church social worker. I owe my religious upbringing due to my mother trying to live up to Aunt Dick's expectations for the family.

We had a little two-tube radio that was powered by a 12-volt battery, a bias battery and accumulator, a glass 1.5-volt battery, that had to go to the store and be charged every week. Due to the fact we only had one accumulator, when it was being charged, we were without a radio, or wireless as we called it.

In time, Dad found a job with a Ford Motor dealer called Moore's, in Weybridge about five miles from Old Byfleet, a job he kept for about ten years until the depression was over. During that period many things happened. It was from that house I first started school and the only three things that come to my memory from that period are; I was sent home from school once because a rumour circulated that my father had a fatal accident which was not true; I was in a school play and couldn't perform because I had mumps; I always remember seeing the Zeppelin R101 fly over very low on its way to nearby Brooklands airport. I climbed on the shed roof to get nearer to it.

When I was about six years old, we moved from Chertsey Road to 201 New Haw Road, about two miles away. That house belonged to my Aunt Lena who was my mother's eldest sister. She had lost her husband during World War 1 and never remarried. She worked as a cook for Lord and Lady Brunker who had a large mansion in Addlestone. Lena was a pleasant, active, easy-going person, and relatively well-off compared to us. I would depend on her for my best Christmas present and the little special things she always brought for me when she visited. One thing I always remember was her chain smoking. My mother hated it, especially if she smoked in our house. There were never ashtrays in our house so she would sit holding the cigarette vertically and let the ash collect in a column, sometimes the length of the cigarette. I can't remember what happened when it fell off, but I believe she caught it in her hand. My father smoked – he rolled his own. I am sure it is due to my mother's attitude towards smoking that I have never been hooked on smoking. I did smoke a pipe now and then for a few years.

New Haw was in a beautiful country area close to a canal and a waterfall we called, "The splash". There were locks within a couple of hundred yards of our house. One or two horses, large like Clydesdales, pulled the barges that ran along the canal. We used to ask the Bargeman if we could ride from one lock to the next, and sometimes we were lucky. Once there was a small barge without a horse and the man was pulling it alone and he let us steer it to keep it in the middle of the canal while he pulled. I must have been about seven so, goodness knows how well we did.

There were beautiful meadows of flowers, woods full of bluebells, blackberries and so many places to explore. I was rarely at home. No wonder I was not very keen on school and preferred to wander. I will always remember one incident. We had just returned from a visit to my uncle and aunt in Dagenham. I was still in my best suit. The moment we arrived home I was off along the canal. Unfortunately, that was the day I happened to fall in. What a mess!! I was frightened to go home. I can't remember what happened. I had many spankings, so it wouldn't have been unusual. I can never remember my father ever hitting me.

My father was still working at Moore's. My mother didn't work outside of the home. She was always there when I came home from school or returned from one of my long days of roaming in the countryside. She was a good, simple cook, and kept a clean tidy house. I always had clean fashionable clothes. I did a few things my mother wouldn't have approved of, but nothing terribly bad. There was always so much to do without causing problems. My mother was good to me in many ways and I am sure she loved me and did her best. She was quite strict and didn't hesitate to spank me if I stepped out of line. One of the worst things that she used as a weapon to make me do her bidding, was threaten to send me away to a boy's reform school. This made me feel insecure. I can remember crying for forgiveness and pleading with her. She hung this over me for a lot of years until I realised it was an empty threat. But I am sure it left its mark.

Without even trying or doing any homework, I always got by as an average student. I don't have very good memories of school. Once I was humiliated in front of the class in second grade by being wrongly accused of stealing a banana from the cloakroom.   Another time we were all sent out to find the longest dandelion stem. When I turned up with the longest by far, I always felt I didn't get the credit that another student would have gotten. I often wonder what caused the different feeling towards me (which I may have imagined). Perhaps it was my London accent! I know I had other kids to play with, but I don't remember having a real special friend I could turn to.

There was a boy named Stanley Smith who lived a couple of doors from me. We got on fairly well together. There was a dog that always followed me everywhere. This was a common thing with me while I was growing up. It was a long time before I would have a dog of my own. I always managed to have a neighbour's dog that took a liking to me, and would follow me everywhere filling my loneliness.

Once when the neighbour dog was following me, I was trying to get rid of him in front of a store about a hundred yards from my home. There was a square post in the area where I was running to get away from him. I looked around at the wrong moment and bumped into the post and finished up at the doctor's office. It was on a Sunday morning and we didn't have a car so we had to wait for the public transportation to have the gash on my forehead stitched up.

As an only child, my childhood was very lonely and many times I would feel as if I had to look entirely after myself and no one cared. I cried myself to sleep many nights when I had done something wrong and feared the consequences.

After living in New Haw for about four years, my parents decided it was time they bought a house of their own. They found a nice semi-detached bungalow with three bedrooms, a living and reception room. It wasn't very large, but had everything we could want. There was a large yard and the rear boundary was the River Bourne, a nice clean fast running river that I really enjoyed. It was good to be able to fish in my own back yard.

There were three tall alder trees in the yard that I frequently climbed much to the distress of my mother, who wouldn't dare to look up at me hanging at the top. There were miles of fields and open country beginning a few yards from my house where I could wander. This was where I spent most of my time. We had a raft on the river that ran at the bottom of the yard and had lots of fun with it, but we swam in another river called "The Wey", that was about two miles from the house. The River Bourne was too cold and shallow to swim. The Wey was one of the best swimming places anyone could want. There were beautiful banks of clean, golden sand that was washed up each winter. And a nice wooden bridge to dive off. The water was clean and usually, fairly warm, and it was in the country where nobody bothered us. I would leave the house at seven in the morning, take a sandwich, and arrive back home at nine in the evening. As usual, my mother used to worry about me more than necessary, or so I thought.

There was also the canal and a large pond about a half mile across within a mile of the house. Everything a young boy could want. Even a mill driven by water. When I was ten or eleven, I stepped into a fire of smouldering corn husks at the mill. It filled my shoes and burnt my feet badly. I had the sense to immediately jump into the pond that was nearby. At that time, it was the theory that you shouldn't put burns in water, but I am sure that saved me from a very serious burn. A little girl who turned out to be one of my future wife's best friends, was also seriously burned and I had to go to court as a witness in a case claiming compensation from the mill for her injuries. I don't remember if they won the case.

It must have been all these attractive places to spend my time that kept me from being interested in my schoolwork. I had a pellet gun and used to shoot at everything that moved. The neighbour dog would find hedgehogs and I would take them home and keep them as pets, feeding them bread and milk. I had white mice in the shed that multiplied and got out of the cage and ran around the shelves at night so when my father came home from work their eyes would shine. Finally, my dad laid down the law, and they were gone.

There was also a big building project close to the house where we used to play. One of our favourite tricks was to take the center out of the large piles of stacked bricks making a fort, then use conduit as a pea shooter with rolled balls of putty as ammunition. We would shoot at unsuspecting workers or other people that went past. It wasn't too long before we were caught at that game and I was in hot water. My mother nagged at me a lot and didn't spare the spanking. I can remember saying to her, "Hit me and stop nagging." I can't remember what the result was of that. I know I had her in tears many times. She continued to threaten to send me to a boy's reform school throughout my growing up. It can be tough when you are the experimental only child or number one and have all the expectations and dreams of parents placed upon you. As a family grows, the parents know what to expect, and can spread their dreams and hopes.

I never seemed to satisfy my mother.

When we moved to Addlestone, I was transferred to a new school, Saint Paul's. It was about a mile from home, and I had to walk it four times a day for the first three years. I can remember playing marbles most of the way home and there were always kids to walk with. Finally, I got a bike. It was a girl's bike that my dad had fixed up and painted for me. He was always good like that. I can never remember him giving me a bad time in any way. He always left it to my mother. I know I used to get into his tools and he told me about that a few times but that was it.

One of our favourite tricks to get home from school quickly was to hang on the back of a truck on our bicycles. We called it a "wippee", and if the truck went too fast, we would let go, of course. One day I hung on until it was too late. The truck sped up and the driver edged over to the curb to get me off. I crashed. I finished up in Weybridge Hospital with badly grazed knees and deep cuts in my elbows. It took six weeks of outpatient treatment to recover from that. I never told the whole truth about what had happened and they tried to find the driver, but never did. Fortunately, I never had any long-term problems from it.

School was quite tough. They didn't spare the cane if anyone talked during class or got out of line in any way. My best subjects were mental arithmetic, and I used to enjoy woodwork once a week during the last two years. The instructor liked me, and I did well. I always did well with things if I got some appreciation and praise.

I was always interested in aeroplanes and wanted to fly. We used to go to Brooklands, a car and motorcycle racetrack with high banks where it curved. The airfield was in the middle and we would watch the aeroplanes take off and land. It was there that I had my first flight. I was about eleven years old. We were at the airfield and I saw an advertisement "Flying one shilling a mile" – about ten cents. "This is it," I thought to myself.

As soon as I got home, I told my parents that was what I wanted to do. I was convincing enough to get a shilling. How? I don't know. It wasn't easy for me to get money. My parents never had it to spare. I offered to get a job but they were always against it. I never had any regular pocket money or work prior to leaving school. The next weekend I turned up at Brooklands at the pilot's flight shed and office with my shilling for the mile flight. There were a number of Pilots standing around in the room and when they heard me ask for the flight, and saw how sincere I was, all dressed up with a cheap plastic flying helmet and my overcoat, they thought it was such a joke one of them decided to take me on a flight. It was in a Puss Moth, a single engine four-seat high wing aeroplane. We flew over Windsor castle, my house and all around. What a thrill! I was walking on air for weeks after that. They didn't take my friend, and it was a shame really, but not my fault.

Finally, at the age of fourteen I left school. I was just a kid no height or size. My dad was able to get me a job at Hawker Aircraft Company. I was so pleased as I wanted to be close to aeroplanes. I was to take an apprenticeship as an aircraft fitter. During that period, I would be given a day off work each week to go to a technical school to continue my education, providing I went to evening classes. My wages were four and halfpence per hour and we worked 48 hours per week.

It was from then on that I realised I needed to get an education to get anywhere.

Chapter 2

WAR TIME

Cadets before I joined the RAF - Early 40s

The war had started by the time I started work and they needed every Hurricane aircraft they could make. It was one of the planes used in the "Battle of Britain". We made three or four aeroplanes each week. I enjoyed working at Hawkers, and did really well at the job. Finally, I was doing something I was appreciated for. I always had good mechanical aptitude and adapted well.

I worked for a guy named Fred Leader. I was an apprentice aircraft fitter working in the flight sheds. I was doing final installations and inspection on the aircraft making them ready for dispatch. I can remember being given the responsibility of fitting the ammunition shoots to the machine guns as well as installing the extended long-range fuel tanks. I worked there for about two years. The guy I worked with was good to me and helped me in many ways. They must have realised I was capable because they moved me around and gave me a lot of responsible jobs. As young and small as I was, I was accepted and treated well by my work mates.

It was during that time we were bombed twice.

The first time was during lunch. A German Heinkel 111 dropped a couple of bombs on the airfield and missed our factory by miles. We were sitting on the grass on the side of an air raid shelter. Without warning, the German aircraft came roaring across the airfield out of nowhere and dropped the bombs across the airfield. We just lay and watched, completely taken by surprise. We tried after to get into the shelter and it was locked. They locked the shelters because they found a couple of workers hiding in there on second shift when they should have been working. Fortunately, the bombs were not near us that time.

The second time we were bombed was later in the war. We were not allowed to respond to the general public warning system. We worked on until the spotters on the roof could see the aircraft and then they operated a manual siren. By then we didn't have much time before the bombs began to fall. We were working when the second raid started at about 10:00 A.M. We really got moving when the siren went. As we ran to the shelter there was hail of machine gun bullets and all the anti-aircraft guns were firing. A squadron of Junker Ju 87 dive-bombers dove at us. I ran as fast as I could to the shelter that was about a hundred yards from where I worked. I just got into it when the bombs began to explode. The explosion blew me into the shelter. They dropped about a dozen bombs and two of them had exploded about sixty yards from the shelter. All together there were about five exploded bombs. The unexploded bombs disrupted production for quite a while. The two bombs that exploded near us missed our plant and fell on Fraser Nash antique car storage buildings that were near the shelter. We were lucky. One of our guys got a bullet in his shoulder. Nobody got killed and they missed our buildings and didn't stop production for very long.

The assembly plant was about a quarter mile from us, so we were able to continue to work while the army engineers defused the unexploded bombs from the assembly area so we could get back to production as quickly as possible.

Brooklands track was a good landmark for the Germans to find even though they had camouflaged it with frame houses to cover the round conspicuous race track. They had built wood frame houses over the track. Then covered them with wire netting. They sprayed feathers with glue over them and then painted them to look like houses. It was still easy to locate from the air. Eventually, they did the right thing and moved the company about ten miles away to Langley. Since I was so young it was further than I could travel. Much to my dismay, that was the end of my working directly on aircraft.

There was very little food at this time. Because of the war we were on very strict rations. The meat ration was about a quarter pound per person per week and two ounces of butter, margarine and sugar. Clothing and shoes were rationed. Fish was only available if you happened to be at the store when it arrived. Bread was available, but there were long lines for it. There was a small allowance of eggs, about two a week. We gave up our egg ration in exchange for a bran ration so the family could get chicken meal and we went in partnership with a neighbour to have enough table scraps and bran to feed them. We then shared the eggs. My dad kept rabbits to supplement the meat ration and most families grew their own vegetables. The children had never seen an orange or banana. They had to be imported and the ships were needed for war supplies and more essential foods. Only people who were on essential work and had to travel a distance with a car full of passengers were able to get petrol (gas). Most good cars were taken and used for war service.

My new job was with a company called Addlestone Engineering and I worked for them as a machinist. I was still an apprentice and I continued my schooling. I was also doing a correspondence course with the British Institute of Engineering.

When I was fifteen, I became a member of the Air Defence Cadet Corps, and used to go to meetings twice a week in the evenings and Sunday mornings. It later became the Air Training Corps (ATC). We had a uniform just like the Royal Air Force, but with a closed collar. Later in the war, it became the government's source of aircrew and mechanics as soon as the members reached eighteen years of age. I was selected to train as Pilot, Navigator or Bomb Aimer. All the time I was a member, I was trained to go in the RAF (Royal Air Force) in one of those categories. We studied Math, Navigation, Metrology, Morse code, Aircraft engines, had drills and everything else related to the RAF and flying. We were given opportunities to fly as a passenger on Wellington bomber test flights from Vickers Armstrong, which I did every chance I had.

My life was busy with no time to get into any trouble or have any teen problems. Sometimes I went to the ATC every evening of the week. I had a good friend named Pat Molin who was a member. By the time I was ready to go in the service I was a Sergeant.

We were experiencing bombing nightly throughout this period. We were now living in Addlestone, about twenty miles from London. We were in line for all the planes heading for the city and got more than our share of the bombs. The sirens would go every night as soon as it got dark and the bombers would start buzzing over, dropping their bomb loads. The anti-aircraft guns would be blasting while searchlights scoured the sky trying to find the aircraft. If they caught one, it would usually drop its load of bombs so it could manoeuvre better to get away. The guns would roar and all hell would break loose for a while.

When it was early in the evening my, dad and I would often go out and watch it all. My mother used to like to go to the public air raid shelter. We had what was called a Morrison table shelter. It was a large steel table with three-inch, angle iron legs, a two-inch angle frame, and one-eighth steel plate on the top. Around the sides was the squared reinforcing wire like they use in cement reinforcing. We had our mattress in that. Since we lived in houses built of bricks, short of a direct hit, it was fairly safe. My dad and I would sleep there when things were really bad.

One night when we were laying in our Morrison shelter, we heard the whistle of a bomb we thought was for us, but fortunately it was not a high explosive bomb but a load of incendiary bombs. A couple fell in the garden, but not near enough to cause a problem. We just let them lay where they fell on the earth and burn harmlessly out. Sometimes they would explode and spray the flammable material around. We called them V1's Buzz Bombs. You would never hear the one that got you. We would hear them buzzing over and sometimes the engine cut off. We then waited until we heard the explosion in the distance. By the time they had glided down they would be well away. They were just trying to destroy the morale of the people. The Germans had little idea where they would land.

When the V2's started, I was in the RAF in London. Nobody heard those until they exploded because they were rockets that came from out of the upper atmosphere beyond detection in those days. Good job the Germans never developed the atomic bomb else it would have been the end of everything for us.

Vickers Aircraft was bombed a few times. One time, 108 people were killed on the night shift. I did not know any of them personally. As I walked to work, I could remember all the glass being blown from the store windows spread across the street. Weybridge School received a direct hit one night. My future wife was attending that school at the time and can remember arriving at school to find all the books in the trees and everywhere. The kids thought it was fine. When they saw the damage, they thought they would be sent home. Instead, the teachers had them picking up the books, and throwing rocks to fill up the crater.

We were lucky and never experienced the destruction and loss that London did. When I visited London with my dad, we saw a lot of damage in the area where my grandmother lived. At least sixty percent of the houses had been destroyed.

My teenage years, including going to technical school and being in the ATC. Completing a course with the British Institute and Engineering Technology was a big plus to my education. It helped develop my attitude and self-confidence, a definite need at that time in my life. Being a member of the Amalgamated Engineering Union, and serving the rest of my apprenticeship with Addlestone Engineering, I became a Union recognised Journeyman toolmaker by the time I was ready to go into the Royal Air Force.

One summer evening, there was an incident that occurred during my ATC, Air Transport Command, service when I was at our headquarters on the Brooklands track. It happened later in the war. Due to repeated bombing, they had installed barrage balloons at Brooklands to deter the dive bombers. We were in a meeting when a Mustang fighter from an American base found himself in the middle of the balloons. He pulled up too steep, stalled and crashed about seventy-five yards from where we were. We thought it was a bomb and ran out to see what was going on and saw the flames and smoke from the crash. We rushed over to the crash site to see if there was anything we could do. We could see the Pilot, but the plane was one mass of fire and too intense to approach. We had to back off. The fire department arrived and sprayed the area with foam to put out the fire.

Certainly, it was a distressing sight to witness.

We frequently had evenings when we would go cross-country running or play soccer. We would meet in an area where it was open country, and go on about a four or five-mile run. Swimming the rivers and enjoying the exercise and each other's company was also a part of our days. We once went on a four-mile, organized road run with over fifty runners and I came in fourth. Our squadron was quite pleased with my effort.

The continuous classes for my apprenticeship training, going to the Air Training Corps every other night, and air raids most evenings, really kept me busy.

Air Defence Cadet Corps, later and still called the Air Training Corps. ATC is a British volunteer youth organization sponsored by the Royal Air Force in the UK.
Bob is third from the left in the front row. He is 15 years old.

Chapter 3

MILITARY SERVICE

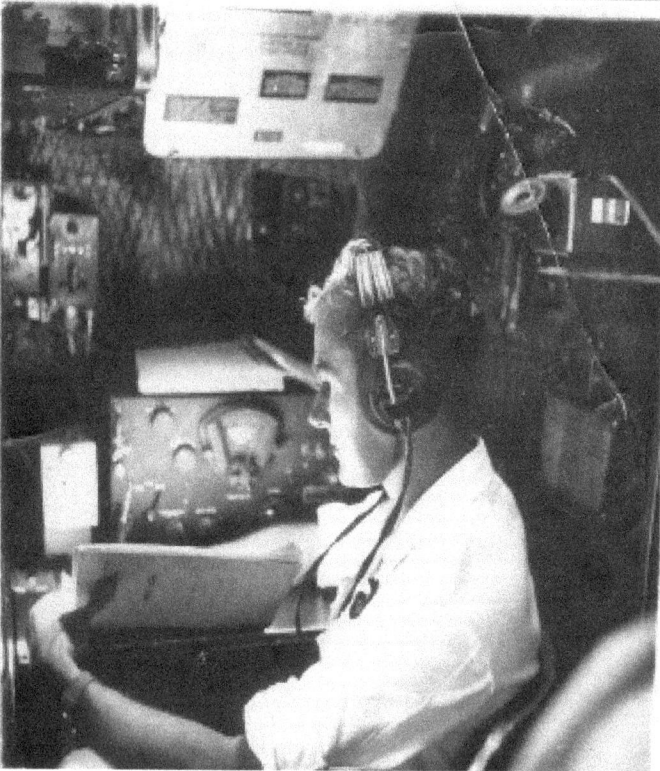

Royal Air Force Aircraft Radio Operator

My main ambition was to be a Pilot, Navigator or Bomb Aimer, which was the goal of most members of the ATC. Finally, at the age of nineteen, I was called to service in the Royal Air Force as aircrew, the only military job that would release me from my reserved occupation, manufacturing essential machine parts for the war effort. I was to report to St. John's Wood, the intake center for all categories of Aircrew at that time. My parents saw me off from Addlestone and when I arrived at Waterloo, I had arranged to meet my Aunt Dick. We met at The Lambeth church and we went together with her minister and had a little service with just the three of us. We asked that I be spared through my service life. It was a touching experience that I remembered frequently throughout my service career.

From there I travelled by underground to St. Johns Woods, an exclusive part of the city. We were accommodated in apartments in an exclusive area near the Lord's Cricket Ground. We had central heating and the bathrooms had heated floors, which was a real luxury for England. The rest of the rooms, except for the kitchen, were bare and empty. An exception was the iron bunk beds on beautiful hardwood floors. At the beginning of the intake process, we were issued our uniforms and had them adjusted to fit. I would not say *tailored to fit*.

Following was the medical check-up. There were so many of us it was a quick listen with a stethoscope, cough, and it was over. That was followed by inoculations and vaccinations. There were hundreds of us. We were lined up for ages, waiting for what seemed like forever. Previous groups had written things on the walls like, "The last flight died waiting" and less discreet messages. We had a cocktail of everything in one injection and that night we had to get on our hands and knees and scrub the floors of our accommodations. I never knew if that was intentional because most of us were not feeling at our best after that vaccination. I was okay, but it was too much for many of the men. Some were really sick.

The next major function of the intake was to select the people who were to continue as aircrew and decide what category they should train as. We were taken to conference rooms at Lord's Cricket Grounds where day after day we took aptitude tests to help them to make that decision. We were also spending a lot of time drilling, having lectures and physical training.

Finally, the time came for the categorisation board's decisions to be announced. The flight, our group of about eighty who had been through the initiation together, were assembled in a large lecture room.

New Uniform - Royal Air Force
1943

At this time, towards the end of the war, very few aircrews were still needed. They were getting selective in deciding who they would accept. We knew a good number would not remain as aircrew. Everyone was on edge pending his fate. When it all ended, there was one straight Pilot, fourteen Pilots/Air gunners, three Bomb Aimer/Navigators, two Wireless Operators, three Flight Engineers and twenty Air Gunners. That left forty-two that did not qualify from the eighty and I was one of the two wireless operators. The other guy had worked at the BBC. Goodness knows how that would have helped make him a better radio operator. The remaining forty plus were to be dropped from aircrew training completely and placed on other assignments. I attribute my ATC training and having learned Morse code to a speed of 14 words per minute, as the reason I was accepted. Although my ambition was to be a Pilot, being a Wireless (radio) Operator was considered a plus. It was while I was there at St John's Woods that the V2 rockets started to land on the city.

The next part of our training was to be the Initial Training Wing (ITW) at a seaside resort in Yorkshire called Bridlington. So, due to the V2's and there being no telling where the next one would land, they got us out of London as soon as possible. It was summer, and it was a beautiful place to move to.

We were to live in private houses almost on the beach. It was perfect except for the strict discipline with lots of drill and physical training. There was a corporal drill instructor who didn't seem to like me, and from what I can remember, he made it as difficult as possible. We were mixed with all categories, so the training was general. We had a very enjoyable time. We were able to go to the Spar Dance Hall on the weekends, and lay on the beach whenever possible. It was like a holiday after having worked in a machine shop for years. We were too far north to be bothered by the bombers, and there was nothing there they wanted to destroy anyway.

At the completion of ITW we were supposed to go to radio school, but again, due to the lack of need for aircrew, we were all sent to other training centers to wait until we were needed to continue training. I was assigned to train as a motor transport (MT) driver, and was sent to Blackpool to do a six-week driving course. Blackpool is the most popular seaside resort on the West Coast and it was the best, with every amusement that could be found at that time. We were in private houses with families right down town. I can picture the older woman we were with. She had two daughters and was as strict as possible. She treated us as if we wanted to accost them if they passed us in the hall. We had to be in at 9.30 P.M. each evening – she wouldn't give us a minute leeway.

There were two of the biggest dance halls in England there, and we could dance every night in a vacation atmosphere. The biggest drawbacks were the 9.30 P.M. curfew, and the lady of the house. Other than that, I had a wonderful time.

The driving course was very intense on every type of vehicle we encountered. At our graduation we were told: "*This course is the best anyone has to offer, and there shouldn't be a vehicle you cannot drive.*"

I remember driving those old Crossly trucks, built in 1926. The gear shift was a lever about two feet long with a handle at the top. The movement to change gears was at least fifteen inches. They had what was known as a crash gearbox. Now all gearboxes are synchromesh. To change up you had to wait in neutral, double-clutch and listen for the engine to slow down before selecting the next gear. To change down was really a work of art. The only way to get it into the lower gear was double-clutch, then accelerate the engine in neutral until the gear speeds matched the speed of the mating gear, then slip it into the lower gear. We would go in groups to drive, and while one of us drove, the others sat in the back on the floor.

One day I saw an old basket work chair in the vehicle yard so I thought I would have something softer to sit on by putting it in the back of the van we were driving in. That worked fine. I certainly had a softer ride. The next morning, when I got out of bed in my lodging, I saw this insect on my arm with a round fat body. I squashed it and it was full of blood. Then I remembered my mother telling me sometimes that basketwork chairs were a place where bugs liked to breed and collect. The next morning before we went out in the van, I looked at the chair and it was loaded with bugs, all big and flat just waiting for the opportunity to feed on a person's blood. That was the only one I saw on me. I only hope I didn't infest our lodging.

After a one week leave in Blackpool, I was posted as a qualified MT driver, but had very little real experience. I was sent to an air base near

Salisbury called Lasham. I arrived there shortly before the invasion, and was assigned to the station MT section. We had to drive the aircraft-crash fire tender. We were a back-up crew to be used in the event of more than one crash at one time, or if the other fire tender was out of commission. As inefficient as we were it was a good job.

The tender had a 300-gallon tank of water, and another tank of liquid called safranine. When the two were mixed together properly it came out as foam, but if not, just as a sludge that would not put out the fire. Sometimes when we practised, it came out as sludge. We had to stand by and watch the aircraft take off and land in case of a crash. Fortunately, we were never needed. That was not our only job. We went into town for supplies and drove passengers to the nearest village, Alton.

There was no social life on camp, so we were quite bored at times. There were other categories of aircrew there. One weekend another aircrew guy and I took a terrible risk and borrowed one of our MT vehicles and went into Alton to a dance. If we had been caught or found out, it would have been the end of our aircrew training and goodness knows what else. Fortunately, we got away with it. We had a good time but I know now the risk wasn't worth it.

One of our many duties was to take care of an airport signal light called a pundit light. We were on duty late one dark and rainy night when we saw a man standing waiting in the rain at the bus stop in front of our building on the public highway. We asked him in. He said he was waiting for his daughter to arrive. He sat down in front of the fire and almost immediately had a heart attack. We did all we knew how, made him comfortable and called the medical officer. They came and took him away and told us we shouldn't have allowed him into the building. For a while we thought we were in trouble again, but fortunately, it all was forgotten and we received a letter from his wife thanking us for helping him.

I was at that base during the invasion June 6, 1944. We saw lots of troops leave for Europe and the front lines. Many never returned.

From there I was sent to a base called Cranwell to get us back into training to do a refresher ITW. It was another place to sort us out and thin our ranks. We had lots of drills; lectures on radio theory;

hours of Morse code; and other lectures related to becoming Wireless Operators. It was an old peacetime air base, the radio school of the RAF for years. All the buildings were brick. There were big parade grounds. The beds were steel slats 1/8-inch-thick and 2 inches wide. On that were 2-inch-thick hair mattresses – not too comfortable for sure. Fortunately, I was only there for about a month.

From there I went to the radio school at a base called Madley near Hereford in the county of Herefordshire. Again, due to the war being nearly at the end and the need for aircrew getting less and less, our ranks were being reduced continuously at every opportunity. I can remember a squadron I was in being cut seventy five percent in one sweep. I must have had a lucky charm because I still hung in. Finally, the war ended in Europe May 7, 1945. As it happened, I was in sick quarters with an upset stomach. I missed most of the celebrations.

Finally, our flying started on a Dominie, twin engine, six seat biplane. With 27 hours flying in Dominies, then 10 hours on proctors – a small single engine mono plane – we graduated and ready to leave radio school. We had been there fourteen months instead of seven, during which time the war had ended. I spent August 14, VJ (Victory over Japan) night in the city of Hereford where everyone went mad and there was dancing in the streets that went on until daylight.

Herefordshire is the part of England where cider is made. Our billets were metal Nissen huts in a cider apple orchard. When the apples were ripe, we used to shake the trees so the apples wouldn't fall on the roof of the hut and wake us up. Cider apples are not good to eat.

The time seemed to go by quickly because there were no big milestones to look back on and gauge it by. We were ready to leave radio school. We had been there fourteen months instead of seven. It was while we were there that I started learning to cut hair. I have a picture of the first haircut I did.

Next, we went to Locking, a camp near Western super Mare on the River Seven, another Seaside Holiday Resort. That course consisted of rifle range, army manoeuvres, and drill and combat training. It included all the requirements to function as a soldier if it became necessary. It was a good course, and the stay in Weston super Mare was enjoyable. I was able to visit Cheddar Gorge, where there were underground caves with stalagmites and stalactites. They were nothing compared with what I was to see in South Africa years later. Weston super Mare had all the entertainment of the other resorts where we had been stationed, so it was another good place to be.

My next assignment was Operational Training Unit (OTU) in Ireland. We went by train via London to Scotland, then sailed by ferry from Stranraer to Larne in Northern Ireland. I travelled on that ferry a number of times. On one occasion, while we were waiting on the deck at Larne for the ferry to sail, we noticed the water was alive with eels and the sea gulls were diving down getting them out of the water. They would stand on pilings with the eels hanging from their beaks and wiggling their body to make the eel go down their throats. Sometimes another gull would grab the other end and they would be flying together with the eel between them. It was an enjoyable wait.

We travelled from Larne to Ardglass by train Via Belfast. On the way, the train had to stop to drive a herd or cows from the track. It felt like real old-time country atmosphere. Our destination was the RAF Airbase called Bishops Court. It was right on the coast, another beautiful place, but this time more remote. Ardglass was the nearest village, a very small herring fishing port with small fishing boats. Their nets hung out to dry while men sat around working on them. We explored the rocky beaches where we could, but unfortunately there had been tankers on the rocks, so there was a layer of black oil all over.

The base was fairly large, with mainly Wellington bombers. This was the plane we were to fly to continue our training. While I was there, I did two flights in an Avro Anson over to Valley, an airbase on the Isle of Anglesey off north Wales. We passed over the Isle of Man. This is where the motorcycle Grand Prix was run, and Manx cats with no tails came from. One thing I can remember on that flight was seeing sparks coming out of the hot air heating system just by my seat. They were really old antique air planes even then. I also acted as second Pilot by assisting with winding the undercarriage down and the flaps (it was a mechanical, manually operated system).

We were at Bishops Court and living in Nissen huts again. One Friday Night we had a Sergeant's mess party. What a big night. We were drinking *Black and Tan*, a mixture of Guinness and mild beer. I got more drunk than any other time in my life. I got out of bed in the middle of the night and had to be taken back as I couldn't find my way.

I was called up in front of the squadron commander the next day for acting unbecoming as a sergeant. I had been sitting on a couch with one of the local girls making a fuss of her, and was seen by the base commander's wife who had reported me. Thank goodness it all blew over.

We didn't do much flying during the six months I was there, but it was a good place to be. I spent many weekends in Belfast and was there on Orangemen's Day. Even then, one could sense the tense feelings between the North and South, but there were no bombs or armed fighting. We also visited Downpatrick to see Saint Patrick's grave. The reason there was little flying was they were moving the base back to England to an airfield called Silverstone. After the war, the airfield was used as a motor racing track.

We were all moved to Silverstone and finally started our flying training. We picked up our permanent crew to fly together on the training missions. We flew on X-Country flights performing bombing, circuits and landings. It was September 1946 when we finally started the training. We flew thirty-seven training missions over the next four months. Our crew consisted of Pilot Officer Barns, Navigator Sergeant Chambers, and Bomb Aimer Sergeant Ward. Our gunner's name was Allen Wright, who was to become a very good friend.

After most of our flights we returned to base except for a couple that landed at Abingdon and Brize Norton. Nothing very eventful. One night we had a riotous party in the Sergeants' mess. Everyone got half drunk. It got out of hand when one person put a pint of beer on his head and bobbed up and down singing. Do you know the muffin man? Do you know his name? Do you know the muffin man who lives down Strawberry Lane? He was pointing to another fellow while he sang. Then it was followed by the next one putting a glass on his head and singing, *Yes, I know the muffin man*, etc. This went on until the whole mess hall was full of people bobbing up and down with pints of beer on their heads. Some were standing on the tables. Glasses were falling and being knocked off and you can imagine the mess.

Towards the end of training we were all moved to Swinderby, an airfield near Lincoln. The runway ran parallel with the main road. When a car came along with bright headlights, we put on our landing lights. Having just returned from a trip, it was there that we were sitting on the tarmac one day running the engines down. The Bomb Aimer had been sitting in the second Pilot's seat, a seat that folded down to give access to the front escape hatch, the Bomb Aimer, and front gunner's positions. The front escape hatch was open, and he had been sitting on his parachute because there was no cushion. As he let the seat down he accidentally grabbed the parachute by the rip cord. The chute fell and immediately opened. It was sucked out the front door and wrapped around the engine, stopping it. We thought we were in big trouble, but it told a good story and were even written up in a monthly book called Happy Landings.

When we did circuits and landings at night, we would take over the aeroplane from another crew without stopping the engines. I remember looking up at the radial engine and seeing the cylinders glowing red and still running. We had a flying officer with us on our squadron who was a big show off. One day the crew got into the plane and he was doing his pre-flight checks when he accidentally pulled the fuel jettison lever. The fuel gushed out. They all had to tip toe away from the aeroplane in case they caused a spark. I don't think he ever lived that one down.

It was at Swinderby where we were given the choice of signing on for three years additional service, or discontinue our training. Our whole crew signed on for the additional time. We were given a civilian suit and one hundred and fifty pounds for signing on. We finally finished Operational Training Unit (OTU) on March 16, 1947 with flying colours and went on leave pending an assignment to a Heavy Conversion Course to be trained to fly on Lancasters.

Again, due to a lack of need of aircrew, we were placed on indefinite leave. I was home not knowing when I would be called back. It was during that leave that I bought my first motorcycle. It was an ex-army 350cc Triumph side valve. I went to pick it up in Ilford, East London with Allen, the gunner on our crew. I had never driven a motorcycle before, so I had to learn going through the city with Allen on the back. You can imagine what it was like. We did wheelies a few times and had a couple of near misses. While going down Commercial Road, which was paved with hard slippery cobble stones, we stopped beside the driver to a double decker bus and the driver said, *"learning to drive the bike mate."* We made it back home right through the center of the city. Before our six weeks leave was over, I was fed up hanging around home with nothing to do, so I got myself a job in a radio manufacturing company to fill in the time. I was anticipating being on leave for months.

Early May I received a return to unit and ordered to report to a station called Lindholm in the Midlands. I had been on leave for about two months. Lindholm was our Heavy Conversion Unit (HCU) on Lancaster Bombers. We started flying mid-May, 1947. After 24 flights we were graduated on to Lancasters and ready to go to our first squadron. It was near Doncaster racetrack.

I had a lesson taught to me about gambling and not to trust my sight. We went to the races and instead of putting my money on the horses, I saw these guys with three walnut shells – I was sure I knew where the pea was. In no time they had three pounds of mine and then disappeared. That was a lot of money that I couldn't afford to lose.

The Squadron we were posted to was 138 Squadron Special duties. Their assignments were dropping spies and people behind enemy lines and similar duties as well as regular bombing missions. We were located at Wyton in Norfolk about twenty miles north east of Cambridge. We went there as a crew and usually flew together. They didn't have Lancasters, but Lincolns, a later version of the Lancaster that could carry a larger bomb load.

The war was over. It was July 1947. We started off with conversion for our pilot to the Lincoln bomber. The Navigator had to learn a new radar called Gee. The mid upper turret changed from four .303 machine guns to two 39 mm cannons, so the gunners were learning new equipment. I don't think the Bomb Aimer had a new bomb sight, but he acted as Navigator on occasions. The radio equipment didn't change. We did lots of circuits and landings and fighter evasive actions that required many hours.

Ground Controlled Approach (GCA) was the system used for landing the plane in poor visibility. Occasionally, we would go over the North Sea for the Gunners to fire off some ammunition. We did long cross-country flights over the continent day and night. One afternoon we set out on one of our routine exercises over the North Sea and were heading back over the Wash, a big inlet north of Norfolk. All of a sudden the plane began to fall out of the sky. It felt as if we were weightless. I wasn't strapped in. My observer parachute was not in its correct stowage and the next thing I knew everything was floating in the air around me, including me. I was up off the seat. The lid of my desk was open. There were rivets and all sorts of rubbish in the air. I thought this was it.

There was nothing to do but wait. I pushed myself up into the astrodome, which was just above my seat. It all happened so suddenly. The next thing I knew I was on my knees as the pilot pulled the aircraft out of the dive. We were lucky. Somehow the pilot was able to get the aircraft under control before we hit the water. I really never knew what caused us to drop, but I know the Bombardier was sitting in the co-pilots seat and they said he was adjusting the trim and all of a sudden, they lost control. When we recovered, we were all shaken up. There were acid fumes and acid coming out of the batteries and everything was a mess. We decided we should head back to base as quickly as possible.

Sometimes at night we would go on search-light co-operation. The lights would try to pick us up. It was strange when they got us. They looked like little flash lights on the ground, yet the plane was all lit up. When they got us, we had to do a corkscrew manoeuvre to try to get out of the beam – Lincoln bombers were not designed for aerobatics. We just went into a twisting dive and sometimes we could shake the light. The bombing range was another of our duties. It was more between the Pilot and Bombardier. I would look out of the astrodome and try to see how well we did. They would phone the score back to the squadron. We usually did okay.

The time was to come when we did the real thing.

I went on one trip called "Operation Sunray". We left Wyton mid-day, flew for 8 1/2 hours to Istres in the south of France, refuelled, then carried on to Castle Benito near Tripoli. We stayed there the night and spent a day in Tripoli. It was my first experience in an eastern country and it was really enjoyable. I saw a lot, took pictures, bought a wrist watch, and had a ball. The next morning, we took off to fly to Shallufa, a RAF base in the desert at the south end of the Suez Canal near the town of Suez – a port and oil refinery. It was warm and pleasant compared to England in November.

We spent a lot of time relaxing in the sun and exploring the area as far as we could walk to places of interest. The Suez Canal was within walking distance of the base, but we had to cross what was called the sweet water canal to get to it. We walked to the sweet water canal and managed to find a raft used by the locals and was able to pay them to take us across. That sweet water canal was used for everything, and it was everything but sweet. It was said if you fell in you would be sent home immediately and goodness knows what you would catch. We never had antibiotics in those days.

We visited the town of Suez a few times. Once when we were there, Allen and I went into the store to buy a watch. He found the one he wanted and we haggled on the price getting the guy down as low as possible. When we got out of the store, Allen looked at the watch and wound it up to find it would not go so we immediately went back inside. The Egyptian fellow would not give us back the money. I looked outside and there were a group of our guys from the squadron going by. I called them over and told them what had happened. They all swarmed into the store. It wasn't long before we had the money back. He wouldn't exchange the watch for one that was working. We must have gotten him down below his lowest price.

A couple weeks later, Allen the Gunner and I decided to hitch hike from our base to Port Said, Egypt via Ismailia, nearly 90 miles. When we were in Ismailia we almost finished up in trouble. We both needed new underwear, and there were some young traders on the street carrying some around trying to sell them. We both brought some off different traders. The only snag was Allen paid the full price where I had really beaten my guy down quite a lot. When the one I purchased from found out he hadn't got as much, he came after me wanting more money and I wasn't about to give him any. He pestered me so much I turned around and knocked all his goods across the road. We saw immediately I had done the wrong thing and that we were in trouble. Allen and I ran as fast as we could with the crowd of kids chasing after us. Fortunately, an army truck came along just at the right moment and picked us up. Goodness knows what would have happened if we hadn't had that stroke of luck.

Earlier, before the underwear event, a kid had come up to Allen and shown him a ring, saying he had stolen it and would sell it cheap. He dragged the stone across a store window and it made a scratch, so Allen thought it was a diamond. I told him, *"Don't buy it!"*, but he did.

When we got on the army truck and looked at it, he realised it was a glint in a brass ring he had paid three pounds for. A lot of money to us then. He just threw it off the truck into the sand.

We continued on our trip to Port Said. Our final destination was Port Toufic. It was on the opposite side of the canal to Port Said. We were going there to meet Allen's neighbour in England. He was about nineteen, and was in the army, and living on an army base in a tent. We spent the night sleeping in his tent. The next morning, we were shown around Port Said for a few hours until it was time to head back. I remember one thing that stands out in my memory. The return trip was enjoyable but uneventful except for driving in a sand storm for part of the way sitting in the back of an open truck and having to cover our faces and mouths to keep the sand out. There was a cholera epidemic in Egypt at that time. We had been inoculated against it so we were not worried, but it did restrict our travel.

Allen and I had brought current passports and civilian clothes with us from England to enable us to travel. We decided we would head for Cairo the following week to see the pyramids. We managed to get passes for the weekend and set off hitch hiking via Suez. An oil truck with an Egyptian driver picked us up. He spoke English and he was a real pleasant guy. It wasn't long before we were halfway there. Then we ran into an army road block. They were checking passports and authorisations-to-travel documents.   Despite all our pleading, we never got past them and had to return to camp. I think the stop was to try to stop the spread of cholera. We didn't get to see the pyramids from the ground as we planned. We did see them from the air when we flew home six weeks later.

The following morning, November 25th, we were called to a briefing and told we were to continue south on a seven-hour flight to Aden. By noon we were airborne heading south over the Red Sea. Our planes had been loaded with 9,000 lbs. of bombs. We were not told anything about the final object of the flight, but the bomb load indicated we were heading for a combat mission of some sort. We landed at Khormaksar an airfield on a salt flat near Steamer Point and Crater at the south end of the Red Sea in Yemen. It was really hot, no air conditioning, just a fan. We were dressed in khaki shorts and jackets. Just by walking a hundred yards at midday made your uniform wet with perspiration. I think it was the hottest, most humid place I have ever been.

We found out on arrival that we were there to bomb the Yemen tribes in the mountains. They had been raiding the camel trains crossing the desert in the area, and it had to be stopped. We dropped 1,000 bombs on them, some delayed action, so one would go off every half hour. The RAF fighter command also had Typhoon fighters strafing the villages with rockets. I felt sorry for the Yemen Arabs in many ways. I sure hope they left the area after our first strike.

On the way back from a raid one afternoon, we were flying low over the desert and passed over a camel train. All of a sudden, the Rear Gunner opened up. I stood up and looked out of the astrodome, which was right by my seat. The Camel Train was running in every direction diving for cover. The Pilot was screaming on the intercom for him to stop, but it was too late. They were far back in the distance by then.

Local towns were Steamer Point, a harbour town and Crater, a town built in the crater of an extinct volcano. When you were in Crater and looked around, the walls of the volcano were all around. We entered the town through a cut out in the wall. It was a hot dirty place. I remember seeing children with a mass of flies around their mouths and noses. It was a place rarely visited by visitors. We arrived and immediately turned around and headed out. I remember seeing one little local boy with the most beautiful, well-kept mop of ginger curly hair. Another baby with a mass of flies around his nose and mouth. We were at Khormaksar for about four weeks. There was little to do at the airport. I remember resting on my bed looking up at the fan – the only way we were kept cool.

Our return to Shallufa was uneventful. We only stayed there for a few days until our return to England. The first leg to Castle Benito was okay. We did see the pyramids from the air. Our take off was delayed from Castle Benito for a day due to a sand storm. We couldn't run the engines with the sand going through them. It worked out well as we were able to go into Tripoli again, which made up for it. I was able to go through the arch at the entrance to the walled old city. I really got the feeling of being in the east. We wandered through the bazaars where there were lots of things for sale. From there it was another nine hours to England. We flew directly to Manston in the south of England, the RAF customs airport. I was a little worried.

While we were on duty out east, we were given a cigarette ration. We were allowed to buy cigarettes cheap. Woodbines came in tins of fifty cigarettes. I didn't smoke, so I had saved my ration and when I knew we were due to fly home, I took all the tins I had accumulated – they were about two inches in diameter. I bound them with black insulating tape making them look like a tube, then affixed them in the bomb bay to look like a part of the aeroplane. It worked. I came home with 2,500 cigarettes, a valuable item in England at that time.

Back on the squadron again with our regular duties, circuits and landings, X-Country flights to other airfields, but always in the UK. Then finally another interesting flight. I was to be on the crew that took the RAF Bomber Rugby team to France. We left for France on June 6th and landed at Bricy Air Base, Orleans and arrived about 12 o'clock. There was a wonderful welcome for us at the airport and we were taken to a nice Hotel in Orleans. After a pleasant meal we were taken to the Rugby field. I wasn't there to play, of course, just crew. We lost the game. Perhaps just as well. There was a big parade and everyone was happy. A banquet followed with plenty of delicious food, wine and everyone was happy and friendly.

When it was over, we went into town with a few members of the French Air Force. We were taken to their usual taverns and introduced to everyone. One of the French men could speak some English and the language barrier didn't seem to be a problem. I can remember walking down the middle of the street with a Frenchman on each side singing *Hay bubba re bub*, having a wonderful time. We finished up at a dance. I remember meeting a young lady and after dancing with her a lot. I asked how she was to get home. She said her father was picking her up in his car. She gave me the impression that no young lady was safe on the street at night. Then finally, at a very late hour, we were taken back to our hotel. It was an evening to be remembered.

The next day at about noon, we took off to return to England. Our Pilot was Wing Commander Munroe, a real show off. He had obviously had a good night and was still feeling the effects. We took off at top speed meaning he held the brakes with the engines at high speed so that when he let go, we would pick up speed as quickly as possible.

As soon as we were airborne, he immediately banked as hard to the left as he could, just above the ground, cutting around right in front of their flying control tower. Crazy, we had a plane full of rugby players

Changi Air Force Base

AIR MINISTRY,

WHITEHALL, S.W.1.

8th July, 194

MESSAGE FROM
THE SECRETARY OF STATE FOR AIR.

You are now an airman and I am glad to welcome you into the Royal Air Force.

To have been selected for air crew training is a great distinction. The Royal Air Force demands a high standard of physical fitness and alertness from its flying crews. Relatively few attain that standard and I congratulate you on passing the stringent tests.

You are, of course, impatient to begin and you naturally ask, "When do I start?" Your order on the waiting list is determined by your age, date of attestation, and so on; and you may be sure that you will not be overlooked when your turn comes.

While waiting, go on with your present job, or if you are not in employment, get a job - if possible one which helps on the war effort.

You will want to know why you, who are so eager, should have to wait at all. I will tell you.

The Royal Air Force is a highly organised Service. In the first line are trained and experienced crews whose stirring deeds and dauntless courage daily arouse the admiration of the world. Behind these men and ready to give them immediate support are the newly-trained crews fresh from the schools. In your turn, you and other accepted candidates stand ready to fill the schools. Unless we had a good reserve of young men, like you, on which to draw, time might be lost at a critical moment and the vital flow of reinforcements would be broken.

I hope this explanation will help you to understand. The waiting period should not be a waste of time. There is much that you can do. You are very fit now or you would not have been chosen. See that you keep fit. Work hard and live temperately. Learn all you can in your spare time about the things you must know if you are to be efficient later on in the air. The more knowledge you gain now the easier it will be when you come to do your training.

In wishing you success in the Service of your choice, I would add this. The honour of the Royal Air Force is in your hands. Our country's safety and the final overthrow of the powers of evil depend upon you and your comrades. You will be given the best aircraft and armament that the factories of Britain and America can produce. Learn to use them well.

Good luck to you!

Archibald Sinclair

SECRETARY OF STATE FOR AIR.

and crew. He could have killed us all. We headed for England.

I did my usual radio contacts and everything went according to plan. Then he asked for a weather report which I provided. The next thing I knew he had turned around and was heading back to France. He had wanted to go to Paris and thought he would use the weather as an excuse to land at Le Bourget so we could spend some time in Paris.

We arrived over Le Bourget and tried to make contact with flying control by W/T, Wireless Telegraphy, and R/T, Radio Telephony, but we didn't have a frequency to get them. After a couple of circuits the Pilot told the Navigator to fire off a red flare on the approach, and we just headed down the glide path, shooting off another flare before landing.

Immediately we got to dispersal and were impounded, surrounded by security. Myself and the rest of the crew were escorted off the aircraft and taken to a briefing room. We were asked a lot of questions, briefed and sent on our way. We started the engines and then were led by a jeep to the end of the runway. That was the end of our hopes for Paris. We landed at Oakington to clear customs and then flew back to our home base, Wyton. I had my logbook showing everything that was said and done to cover me and I didn't have any problems, but I was told Wing Commander Munroe was really in trouble, and may have lost his commission. There were a number of senior officers in the rugby team who were not too happy about what had happened.

While I was at Wyton I signed up at Cambridge Technical College and spent one day a week studying Math and English. I did learn something, but due to frequent flying duties disrupting my classes, I did not get as much out of it as I had hoped. I volunteered for a special study at Cambridge University, something to do with hearing. While I was there, I was able to go to Marshals Airport just out of Cambridge and fly in a Tiger Moth. I did quite lot or aerobatics like looping the loop and slow rolls, etc. That was fun.

Allen was playing with fire at Wyton for a time. Somewhere in London, he had met this attractive young woman named Laura. Her husband was an officer in the RAF and she was separated from him. It worked out that the husband came to be Allen's chief Gunnery Officer when we got to Wyton. That was okay, except that she decided to go back to the husband to be near Allen. She arrived at the camp and moved in with her husband. It wasn't long before she was wandering around the base so she could meet up with Allen again. She used to have this big white German shepherd with her, that and her being so attractive, everyone knew her. Sometimes she would stand and talk to Allen at the window of our barracks. Allen and her would go off on weekends together and he would take all sorts of risks. He never got found out as far as I knew. He must have had a charmed life.

I was frequently bothered with losing my voice and sore throats, so while I was at Wyton I went to Ely Hospital and had my tonsils removed.

Both Allen and I became restless for something other than being on the bomber squadron and decided to see if we could get a transfer, Allen to coastal command and me to transport. When Allen was not deployed, he worked in the Air Ministry Personal posting department, so he knew all the ladies who looked after the location of aircrew. One weekend, when we were on leave, we took a visit to the Air Ministry to see the people he used to work with. We told them of our plans and asked what they could do for us. The lady said she thought she could help us. She took our names and numbers and asked details of where we wanted to go and said, "I can fix that for you".

About three months later (I had almost forgotten our visit) instructions arrived from Air Ministry for our posting for training to two different commands. Unheard of, but it went through like clockwork, and it wasn't long before we were on our way. Before we were due to report, we were both given two weeks leave, so we had an opportunity to have some time together.

One weekend we decided to have a night out in the West end of London. Allen had brought a white Triumph Gloria Vitesse, a fancy conspicuous car. We spent the evening wandering around different night clubs and finished up in a bar. We were discussing our evening and mentioned it was a shame we hadn't found a good one. There were two navy guys in civilian clothes there that overheard us. We got talking to them and they told us they knew of a good place and would show us where it was. We all got into Allen's car and headed for the East End where the club was. On the way, we needed to stop to use the rest rooms, and while we were out of the car, we heard a crash of glass breaking. Looking back we remembered that there were two or three ladies of the night hanging around where had the car parked. Thinking nothing of it we proceeded to the nightclub.

We hadn't been in the club for long before the police were in there and arrested us. We were being taken in for breaking and entering. Allen had to follow one police car and there was another behind us. They took us to the West End Central Police Station. They asked us a lot of questions and we finished up in a cell. About 6:00 the next morning, they came in and told us we could go. We were out of there as quick as lightning asking no questions and headed back to Allen's house.

Turns out the two navy guys had broken into a liquor store when we had stopped and must have confessed it to the ladies. That is the nearest I have ever been to spending time in jail.

When our leave had finished, Allen had to report Pembroke Dock to the Coastal Command gunnery school and I went to Bircham Newton for my conversion to American radio equipment training and introduction to transport command. The planes we were to fly were Dakotas or Douglas DC3's, good, well-proven old timers. I think there was more of that model made than any other transport plane at that time. It was used mainly as a transport and passenger plane, but it also served for paratroops and supply dropping and glider towing.

While we were at Bircham Newton they demonstrated the plane's ability to snatch a glider from the ground from a standing start. The glider was on the ground with a long tow line with a loop that was held with poles. The tow plane flew low with a hook on the end of a long cable. A winch in the plane hooked the loop and took the glider in tow. In a way it was a very dangerous operation only done by specially trained pilots. They wouldn't let any of us be in the plane or the glider. They also used to pick people from the ground the same way, like spies in enemy territory.

We were trained on American Liaison radio transmitters and receivers as compared to the 1154 and 1155 English Marconi equipment. We did not fly from Bircham Newton. We were moved to North Luffenham for our flight training and to pick up our new crew. My Pilot was Flight Lieutenant Taylor, but I don't remember who the Navigator was.

When we were halfway through our training, the Berlin air lift started. That was when the Russians bottled up Berlin and all the supplies had to be flown in. We were unlucky as we were one flight short of being trained enough to be part of it, so we had to wait around because they had taken all our aircraft. We just did odd jobs, including preparing a grass tennis court for the officer's mess. I did okay because having done an MT course, I got to drive the roller while the other guys raked and dug. We could see the officers sitting in their mess while we worked. So just for fun, we collected dandelion seeds and planted them all over the court. I couldn't complain.

We played a lot of Bridge in the Sergeants' mess and really had a relaxing time including getting some extra leave. When the airlift was over and we continued training, we did about 40 flights and 90 hours to complete our conversion course. Our next course for the whole crew was Army co-operation training. Due to the radio operator having the extra duty of being Jumpmaster, we had to go to parachute jumping school for a week, missing a week's leave. The course was at Upper Heyford, the parachute and supply drop training station of the RAF. The number of jumps we were to get on the course depended on the weather and the serviceability of the Aircraft.

There was a towers that took an open parachute up with a person on and dropped them. But that was not in our syllabus so we didn't get that for a start. We started the training learning about parachutes, how they were made and packed, and their size for various uses, etc. That was followed with instructions on the harness and safety expectations. We then went to the hangers where we spent a lot of time learning to fall and roll to minimize the impact of landing. There was a high platform with cables at various angles. It went down to a mat to reduce the impact of landing. We were fitted into a harness at the top of the wire that had a pulley so the harness would run down the wire to simulate a parachute landing. They were able to start the student off slowly and increase the speed of landing until they thought it was safe for each person to do an actual jump.

We missed a day due to weather, then everything was a go and suitable for jumping. We could not jump with a wind speed that exceeded 6mph. Finally, a good suitable morning came to do our first balloon jump. There were five of us and the Jumpmaster all fitted with chutes and waiting to go. It was a cool damp morning with a light mist across the fields. The balloon was the type used for barrage balloons. It was tethered to a truck with a cable to a power operated winch with a basket hanging down with cables attached.

This was it!

We all were able to get into the basket, which was not actually a basket, but a square box with an opening at one end with a rope and hook across it. Up we went. It was silent except for a slight wind noise. The handling ropes on the balloon were at a slight angle due to the breeze. We stopped at 800 ft, everything seemed to go quiet except for the Jumpmaster's voice. "Everyone hook up your static line", he yelled. We all hooked to the rail in the center. I am not sure who went first, but I remember standing at the door looking down seeing all these little people running around. The trees were poking up through the slight mist. The next thing I knew was stepping off into space. The static line – a line attached to the box and the ripcord that pulled the chute open – was open in no time, and I was floating down. There were instructors on the ground instructing us on landing: "Get your feet together!" "Bend your knees!" In no time it was over. My first jump. I don't remember the second in any detail, but I know it was approached with much more confidence.

There was only one day left for us to get an aircraft jump in, and it was a long weekend coming up. The crew of the aircraft found a way to say the plane was not serviceable, so it never happened. I just had to think myself lucky we got the balloon jumps. Lots of people did the course and didn't get to jump at all.

The next course we had to do was Army Corporation. We did two months of glider towing, supply and Paratroop dropping. It was interesting, and we did a lot of flying. We were shown how to get a Paratrooper back in the aeroplane when his chute is hooked on the tail wheel. Also, we were instructed on how to handle a person who refuses to jump. We had to lock them in the toilet. Because they sometimes changed their minds and have been known to jump after their static line has been disconnected. We were being trained to go to Malaya. English Paratroopers didn't jump with a spare parachute.

We left from Portsmouth in early February 1949, heading for Singapore. It was about dusk when we left port. It was the first time I had been on a large ship. Our sleeping quarters were in a hammock that was strung across the table where we ate. None of us had ever slept in a hammock before, so it was quite a pantomime seeing everyone trying to get themselves set up. The only cover we had was one blanket. The weather was really cold and so was the temperature where we slept.

Some of the men decided it was better to sleep on the table and deck sooner than in the hammock. Everyone was freezing cold and had no way to get warm. If we had known our way around the ship, perhaps we could have found somewhere else.

When we reached the Bay of Bisque, it really got rough and a lot of the guys were seasick. It was a mess. As well as RAF there were Navy personnel on board, and it was their first time at sea. Prior to us setting sail, they were strutting around in their navy uniform looking smug, so to see them hanging over the side or over a bucket was amusing.

Finally, we got into the Mediterranean and some calm, warmer weather. Everyone began to enjoy the cruise. We stopped at Port Said, and then at Port Sudan about halfway up the Red Sea on the east African coast. That was the one and only time I ever went ashore there. It is not a port the cruise ships visit. I remember they were loading a ship with coal by a long line of natives carrying it in baskets on their heads across a gangplank, dumping it on board one basket at a time. The natives there were called the Fuzzy Wuzzies, most likely a derogatory term. They had a mass of tightly matted curly black hair and carried long curved two-edge knives on their belts. I had one of their knives for a long time, but it disappeared. There was a shanty town made of flattened rusty oil drums. I have pictures of the town and can picture it now. From there we didn't go into port until we reached Ceylon – now called Sri Lanka – the port of Colombo.

We sat in the harbour for a long time, then finally went ashore for the afternoon. At that time the major export was tea, but I was going in the wrong direction to buy that. I brought three, semi-precious stones called zircons, which I still have and have never had mounted. We arrived in Singapore and I was taken to my new home for the next two years.

The airbase in Malaya was called Changi. It was located at the north end of the island. I was stationed with a 230 Transport Squadron. I was the only new crew member to arrive at the time. I was given a couple of days to get settled and look around the base. It was a beautiful place with a golf course, swimming area, yacht club, and everything anyone could want. I became a member of the yacht club and learned to sail. We would go out and sail on the Strait of Johore, the water between Singapore Island and the mainland. I passed my test, and obtained a Helmsman's certificate so I could take any of the boats out. We would go out and visit a couple of the islands, sometimes race. It was the best.

Our living accommodation was in a large cement building, all open to the outside with a big veranda around. There were no malaria mosquitoes, but we used to sleep with mosquito nets all the same. Occasionally, one would get in the mosquito net and it sounded like an aeroplane buzzing around.

The temperature was perfect. We were dressed in shorts most of the time and were comfortable. When we were flying, we had white one-piece overalls with our rank and flying emblems on. They really looked good and were practical. Our flights from Changi varied. We had our regular trip to Labuan, an island off the coast of north Borneo. We sometimes stayed overnight in the Government Rest House. It was a large thatched building that was very cool and pleasant. We would wander around the Island and explore. There was a large war cemetery that was kept immaculate with the grass cut and trimmed with a number of flags flying in the middle. It was strange to see it so well kept and so far from everyone who had someone there and so few people to see it. I wonder if it is still the same.

There were a couple of abandoned Japanese aeroplanes and some beautiful scenery. I was there a number of times. Another of our regular flights were to Changi, Saigon and Kai Tak (Hong Kong). Once on our return form Kai Tak, we had the French Soccer team on board as passengers. The seating was on each side facing each other and the seats folded up when not in use. We were between Kai Tak and Saigon and flying in some rough weather when all of a sudden, we were caught in a down draft and the plane just dropped. I looked out the back to see how our passengers were doing and they were all hanging from the side of the aircraft by their seat belts. The seats had just been folded in position and not secured to the floor so when the weight went off them, they folded under. Fortunately, no one was hurt and we all had a good laugh about it. I don't think any of those Frenchman ever showered, just put on perfume to hide the smell. It was a long time before we could forget their presence. It was extremely hot at times, sitting in an aircraft on the ground with no air conditioning.

We were returning from Hong Kong with a service man with a brain tumour being taken back for an operation. While we were on the ground for refuelling at Saigon, the fire engines sprayed our aircraft with water to keep us cool. Occasionally, we went to Kuala Lumpa. They mined pewter with high-pressure hoses, a coal mining procedure, in Butterworth, further north on the Malaya main land opposite Penang, an Island on the West Coast. We stayed at Butterworth one night and went by ferry to Penang to wander around town. We found a dance hall and it was one that you had to pay to dance with the hostesses. I bought tickets and had to ask the girls to dance then give up a ticket to go on the floor. They were all local Malayan girls. It was good to dance a couple of dances.

There was no dancing at Changi. We slept in straw huts at Butterworth and one of the RAF guys there had a monkey as a pet. The Gurkhas Indian troops would go into the jungles to find the bandits, and we had the job of dropping supplies to them. They would cut down a square of trees to make a clearing, then light four fires so we could find them and drop their supplies. We flew really low, and the bales were on rollers so we would just push them out when we were over the area. We never had any reports of us missing the target.

One of our aircraft hit a tree and came back with a big dent in the front spar. He was fortunate that he was able to maintain control and didn't crash. We did lose one plane and crew. It was a terrible jungle to crash in. The trees were high and large, and it was impossible to make a false landing. Even if you did, the chances of surviving the crash and being found or being able to live in and on the jungle in the humid climate was extremely small.

We were returning one day from a supply drop with another plane and the pilots flew too close and touched the wing tips, breaking a navigation light. Another time we were doing an army cooperation exercise with two jeeps loaded in the plane. The object of the exercise was to see if we could land as close behind the lead aircraft as possible. We were just over the perimeter track and I was watching the Pilot bring it down when we got in the slipstream of the lead aeroplane and it was touch or go whether we crashed or not. Other than those two occasions, I was not involved in any mishaps while we were in the Far East.

One of my favourite trips was to the Nicobar Islands off the end of Sumatra. There was a weather station on an island called Car Nicobar, a little green jewel surrounded with a golden beach and a coral reef making a white foam ring around the outside. There were fourteen Airmen manning the station, and we had to supply them and transport them to and from. We had a couple of instances there during visits that were interesting.

Once there was a real big snake wrapped around a toilet. The natives played the RAF at soccer barefoot. A large sailing boat came in to unload. It had a jeep on board that had to be taken off. There was no dock so they placed two long poles under the wheels sticking out at the back and front and the locals waded out up to their necks and with the poles on their shoulders carried the jeep off.

Our fuel supply there was not stored in a large special tank but in five-gallon drums. I don't know if we always refuelled when we landed there, but this time we did and they had to fill us using the five-gallon cans. One of the pre-flight checks is to turn on the bleed cock at the lowest point on each tank to check for water. When it was done this particular time, the water never stopped. There had been so much condensation in the cans the water was excessive. The water kept on coming instead of fuel. They had to completely drain the aircraft tanks and refill them. There was so much water. After the refill, it was a lot better, so we ran the engines well, checked again then took the plane on a test flight before we loaded up our passengers. We were always cautious when we re-fuelled there after that.

The Nicobar Islands are not accessible to tourists any more. I was told this when we cruised near them on a cruise ship heading for Thailand in 1996. One afternoon we were sent on an air-sea rescue exercise. We were taken out into the China Sea a couple of miles off the coast. Four of us were put into a life raft. The idea was to drop equipment to us called Lindholme Gear. It was four canisters filled with survival equipment for the people in a life raft to help with their rescue. A plane flew over and was supposed to drop the equipment up wind so we could paddle to it. They dropped it a bit too far away for us to get to it. Paddling a round rubber raft is quite difficult. In the process of paddling, one of us managed to put our foot through the bottom of the raft, so we were sitting in water. Then a squall came up and the visibility was down to next to nothing, so it was a disaster. The air/sea rescue boat that took us, soon found us, and picked us up. By that time, we were really cold and wet. That night we were on a night cross-country flight and when we returned and were descending, I had to ask the Pilot to descend slowly. My ears were so plugged I was in pain. This resulted in me having a bad sinus infection for a couple of weeks resulting in having to have my sinus punched and drained in a Singapore army hospital, an experience I wouldn't wish on anyone. I won't go into detail.

In May of 1949, there was a need to transfer twelve Spitfire fighters from Sembawang, Singapore to Hong Kong because the Communist Party was overrunning China. Due to the short range of the Spitfire, it was not possible to fly direct to Hong Kong, so it was necessary to fly in steps using a Transport Command escort of Dakota's.

I was crew on one of the escort planes. We flew from Sembawang to Kuching, Borneo, where they had a perforated steel plate runway. A runway made of perforated plate that was linked together and laid on soft soil to provide a temporary landing strip. We had been there before and stayed so it was not new to us. One of our Spitfires unfortunately dropped a wheel off the edge of the runway when he landed and as soon as it got into the soft soil he flipped and finished up on his back. Lucky for him he was almost out of fuel and there was no fire. He just hung there in his harness until they got him out. He flew with us for the rest of the way to Hong Kong.

Our job was to carry supplies and go ahead to radio weather reports back to the Spitfires and other general duties. We refuelled the planes the first day at Kuching, and then flew on to Labuan. We set up tents and all stayed overnight. Our next stop was unscheduled. Due to range problems, we had to make the extra overnight at Porta Princessa, a small island west of the Philippines. It was a real beautiful tropical setting with palm trees all along the side of the runway. We were treated really well there with a special meal of what I thought was cold pork that turned out to be fish. We stayed overnight in thatched huts and had a good evening of entertainment by the local people.

The next morning, we were up early and on our way without incident to Clark Field, a large well-established American base, but no longer in use because of a volcano spreading ash and causing floods that destroyed the buildings and runways. The night we stayed at Clark Field, we went into a small town called Angeles and bowled at a bowling alley. Some of the guys visited the local bars. I knew American Dollars were at a premium in Hong Kong, but they would only let us exchange seven dollars, which I did. The next morning, we took off to Hong Kong safely escorting the remaining eleven aircraft. I remember sitting in our aircraft waiting for the fighters to get away before we could take off. It was like sitting in a tin can in the blazing sun. Our flying suits were dripping wet. We couldn't wait to be airborne. The fighters were to be there to show a little strength and support for the Hong Kong area. The rest of the crews were sent back to Singapore. We and our aircraft and crew were kept in Hong Kong on standby waiting to remove the British Consulate Staff from Canton White Cloud airport, if necessary.

I had a visa to enter China put into my passport. We stayed there for about six weeks but never did pick up the consulate. We spent our time flying the area and calibrating their new radar equipment that was located at the top of a local mountain called Tian Shan. As a reward, we were taken on a visit to the radar station up a long winding dirt road to the top. The station was the highest point, and they could cover the whole area. As we sent back our location, they could mark our position on their screens to draw a map. There was a beautiful view of the whole area from the top. We had some wonderful times in Hong Kong. It was a bustling, living city compared to the London I had known with no lights due to the blackout and the destruction.

Our money went a long way. All the things not available in England were in abundance there, like cameras etc. I had an account with The Chartered Bank of India and wrote a cheque for a camera. The cash was never taken from my account due to the Chinese currency being so weak. Cheques written for sterling were being used as currency. I heard it was happening but never took advantage of it. The camera was the only thing I got.

There was a Coastal Command Air base on Singapore Island called Seletar where they flew flying boats called Sunderlands, a very large four-engine plane. The radio equipment was British Marconi, which I was familiar with. Due to a shortage of radio operators on one of the squadrons, and the fact I was due to return to England in a short time, I was transferred to 110 Coastal Command Squadron to help them out. I did a few familiarisation flights and it wasn't long before I was familiar with the English equipment again and one of their regular operators.

Taking off and landing on water was new to me, and quite a nice change. Being a large four-engine aeroplane, they had so much more room. We even had a galley and used to cook and make tea. Our duties were similar to the 230 Transport Squadron with the supply dropping etc., but we had bombing capabilities, so that was a change. The bombs we dropped were small, and we had to load them on the racks that slid out under the wing. It became quite hard work lifting the bombs up and hooking them on the racks. Fortunately, we didn't do it often.

I was selected to be the radio operator to go on tour with the Commander in Chief of the Far Eastern Air Force, Sir Hugh Lloyd. We flew from Seletar to Brunei Bay, Borneo. We waited in the bay while he visited the Sultan of Brunei, then on to Jesselton (now known as Kota Kinabalu) in north Borneo before returning back to Seletar. Sir Hugh Lloyd thanked us for taking him there.

A few days later we had an emergency rescue mission. A sailor on a merchant ship 250 miles out in the China Sea, had acute appendicitis and needed emergency treatment. We flew out, found the ship and landed. There was a heavy swell and we were instructed that we could knock off one of our wing tip floats upon landing. As soon as the aeroplane stopped, we were to run out on the opposite wing to make sure that the remaining wing float was the one that settled in the water. Fortunately, we didn't knock off a float.

We had a doctor and nurse on board. Once we landed, the ship sent out a lifeboat and took them. The name of the ship was a tanker called the Pecos. When we returned, we were celebrities and were greeted by the Malaya Tribune newspaper who took our pictures. We were on the front page.

My two years in Singapore were finally over, and it had been enjoyable. I was now on the ship going home. It was August 1949. The cruise home was a nice rest. We would watch the dolphins playing around the bow of the ship. We played bridge, visited Ceylon again, and a few other ports I had been to before. I amused myself cutting hair on deck, a skill I had acquired during my service, and was much better now compared to my first attempt at Madley. I used to enjoy it. I could do a fairly good job but I remember one army guy I was cutting his hair and just couldn't get it right. All my line of customers slowly disappeared, but I had done my best and taken his shilling. I never went on deck at night alone for a while after that.

We had an airman on board who had disc deterioration in his spine and was in the ship sick quarters. It was discovered that ants had crawled up the leg of his bed and got into his cast. They had no way of replacing the cast so they drilled holes into it and sprayed in DDT to kill them. Then they stood the bed in four coffee cans of kerosene

Whatever medical problem people had in that climate seemed to develop more quickly than at home. I had a sinus problem due to that air/sea rescue exercise, and I flew after that with a stuffed-up head. It was due to the lack of antibiotics that I had to have it punched and drained.

Chapter 4

CIVILIAN LIFE & MARRIAGE

It was good to be back in England to be able to go out dancing and see my parents and friends. It wasn't long before I was demobilised. I was given my severance pay and another demobilisation suit, everything including underwear. It was quite a nice outfit. There were a lot of blue pinstripe suits that you could identify as demobilisation suits, but I got a light wool suit that I was happier to wear.

Things were much the same at home. The post war employment boom was in full swing. As a toolmaker, I had unlimited opportunity for work. After a few weeks' vacation, I started looking for employment and putting in applications. I finished up working for Weybridge Machine Tool Company. I had sold my old ex-army, motor bicycles, and brought a new Triumph 350-cc twin, really the top of the line. There was a waiting list in all the stores for bikes and because it was more expensive and not as much in demand, I was able to get it.

I was enjoying single life, going out dancing a couple of times a week. Also, going on weekend trips to the coast and the motorcycle races at scrambles and road racing on the unused airfields. I had plenty of friends and things were going quite well.

I met Mavis, the girl I was to marry. We spent a lot of time on the bike and dancing together. Things were going quite well at work. Motorcycles were the things among the younger group at those times, and we certainly took liberties on them. I was never involved in an accident myself, but lost a couple of friends and one was seriously injured. It would be interesting to see how many of them are still living.

Mavis and I went together for approximately two years. During the last year we never missed a day without spending time together one way or another. We were really in love and enjoyed every minute.

Mavis and I dating

By then I had sold the Triumph and had a 500cc Matchless, a larger motorcycle. We were always on it going here and there; dancing, swimming, walking and everything courting couples do. Mavis was working in an animal research laboratory taking care of the goats and she really enjoyed her work. I was working at W.H. Henshalls at the time, still tool making. I stayed with them for a long time. My parents had moved to a new bungalow at 50 Scotland Bridge Road, in New Haw. My Dad was working for Woking City Council as a maintenance man, and was happy at his work. My mother kept house.

Dad and motorcycle

Mavis' dad was a foreman painter at Weymann Motor Bodies. Her mother worked at Peto Scott Company, a radio manufacturing company. We lived about a mile apart when I lived in Addlestone, but New Haw was about four miles from Addlestone. We decided to get married, told our parents, and there was no problem. Housing was in short supply, but while I was in the RAF, I had saved a reasonable amount of money, and we bought a house before we were married.

Our wedding in Addlestone Church, England - September 1952

We were able to move in after the honeymoon. We were married in Addlestone Church and had a reception of about forty people, mostly relations and a few friends. It was a typical wedding where everyone was reserved and polite, but the families kept to themselves more or less. Later, when I did wedding photography, I was to attend so many weddings – they were often the same way.

Bob and Mavis Wedding, Addlestone Church

Our house was on the same street as my parents, not that we had wanted it that way, it just happened to be the one at the right price and it suited our requirements. It was a three-bedroom, semi-detached brick house with a tiled roof. We had to do a lot of redecorating and fixing, but it was a good sound place and we got a reasonable deal. I always remember it had wisteria climbing all over the front and side which I thought was really good and distinctive and must have taken years to grow and train. Under pressure from the families, I cut it all off, much against my will.

Where we lived on Scotland Bridge Road in New Haw, England

I was still working at Henshalls. I sold the motor bike and brought a little car, an Austin Seven Ruby Saloon. For a while, Mavis worked for a family at St. George Hills for Count Duna Onoff. I can't remember what she did. We were married on September 6, 1952. There were still shortages from the war up to then. We enjoyed being together and having our own house and freedom.

Carole, our first, was conceived about the middle of the next year and we were very happy. She was born in February 1954.

Carole Scanes

We enjoyed the little Austin. It was so different to a bike of course, and I was getting older and softer. I had taught Mavis to drive it so we could share the driving. I remember once she was riding the clutch and smoke started coming up through the floor. With the baby due we decided it was time to trade up to a fancier and more suitable car, so we bought a Standard Eight. I did a lot of mechanical work on it and my new father-in-law painted it for us. It felt like we had a new car.

My parents house and where I lived in New Haw on Scotland Bridge Road. Carole is at the gate with my dad and mum in the driveway. 1957.

My parents lived at 92 Scotland Bridge Road, New Haw, Surrey, and we lived at 50, so we were not far apart. Mavis' parents were living in Addlestone on Shakespeare Road, about 4 miles away. Mavis' dad and my dad helped us fix up the house. We had a nice garden with fruit trees and a half dozen chickens.

There was no central heating in the house. Each room had a fireplace to burn coal. In winter it was a very cold place. We would sit huddled over the fire trying to keep warm. In the morning I would dash from bed to the kitchen, turn on the gas oven and sit and eat my cereal with my feet on the open oven door to keep warm, but that was England. Very few houses were warm and few had refrigerators.

We were still recovering from the war. To get to work, about four miles by road, I usually took a short cut on my bicycle along the river over a foot bridge, which I had to carry the bike over, down the river bank and over a ditch, then across a field. One cold morning riding along the canal path my wheel caught in a rut on the frozen ground and I went sprawling into the water, bicycle as well. What a sight. I was soaking wet. The wheels of my bike had weeds tangled in them. When I arrived back home, I knocked on the door. Mavis was still in bed. She came to the door and we had quite a laugh. I was soon changed and back on the bike and heading off again. I don't think I was even late!

Life was fairly routine. Mavis and I got on quite well together. I had started a part time photography business called Woodham Photographic. I got a business licence, put a display case up in front of the house, and was really busy doing weddings and portraits in the home. It was an interesting experience.

One thing that I will always remember is the atmosphere at the wedding receptions, the way the families seemed to keep apart and relations were strained ninety percent of the time. I had two difficult weddings for photography that I remember, both in Chertsey.

One was where the church door was on the main street and there was only a narrow side walk. It was a busy Saturday afternoon. I had to get the main group arranged on the side walk with people walking past. We stopped the traffic while I took the photos.

The other difficult wedding was another big group. There was very little room between the church and the railing, and it was late in the afternoon getting dark and starting to snow. Fortunately, I had good flash equipment. I was always pleased to see a good exposed film when I opened the developing tank. I used two and a quarter square film for all my weddings. Most of the local photographers used 35mm so I had an edge on quality.

Henshalls, where I worked, was owned and run by three Brothers, Oswald, Dudley & Cecile. Oswald didn't have much to do with any of the employees, but because I was into photography he would often come and have a long talk with me and we got on well. Dudley used to do development work like making a cabinet for the stewardesses to keep the food trays in. He would sketch the part and I used to design and make the tools to produce what he wanted. Cecile never came into the shop much. Anyway, things were okay there and the guys I worked with were good friends. Then we had a strike. What for I don't know!

But as a member of the Amalgamated Engineering, I was on the picket line. It really cooked my goose, and did myself ten times more harm than good. I don't remember doing anything out of the ordinary, but whatever I did, it destroyed my rapport with the brothers. One of the lessons I learnt in my life. I never made a fool of myself again with unions.

There were still shortages even though the war had been over for a number of years. There were no new cars available for the general public to buy. Lots of imported foods were not available. Then the Egyptian crisis was on and they sank ships in the Suez Canal. That almost put us back to wartime rationing again because so few supplies were being shipped in from the south. Our petrol was put back on ration and things were just like wartime all over again. Yet the war had been over for seven years. The general public were up in arms and everyone was talking about getting away from England. Emigrating to anywhere. We were young and had no real ties so we considered all the possibilities and decided Canada would be our best bet.

We lined up at Canada House in a line about one hundred and fifty yards long. Obtained all the forms and got to work trying to make it happen. After all the formalities, I went to Canada House for the final interview. We were accepted and I had found a position with Atomic Energy of Canada as a machinist in Ontario. We were ready to go. The next problem was to get a berth on a ship or a flight. England was being deserted and there were no cabins or seats available. We ended up on an Italian ship called the Castle Felice sailing from Greenock, Scotland. We got the last berth!

Looking back, I realise I was young and selfish taking the only grand children away from the old folks. My Mum wasn't well. She had recently had an operation for cancer and her health was uncertain. I always felt a lot of guilt related to my mother. Perhaps I was running away. It was tough to leave the families for Mavis and for me. Both of our families were in agreement with us leaving, and did not want to stand in our way. Mavis' parents had already lost one son to New Zealand.

Sadly, I was never to see my mother again.

Chapter 5

IMMIGRATION TO CANADA

Saying goodbyes to Mavis' family in England.

There was a lot to do before we could leave Scotland Bridge Road. We had done a lot of work on our house. It was fully furnished, including some very modern Scandinavian G Plan Furniture. There was a beautiful dining room set and other cherished things we had collected. To get things down to a couple of suitcases was not easy. My tools were heavy, but essential. We had to get the tools to Charring Cross-train station because they were too heavy for us to carry, having

Carole with us. We arranged for me to take the tools to the station in a van owned by the green grocer, who was a friend of Mavis'. He was a really big tough, gruff man, and when we got to the station, he just pushed to the front of the ticket window lineup and no one dared challenge him. I made out like I wasn't with him. The tools were to go directly to the ship.

We traveled north to Scotland in the Flying Stockman, as the train was called. We made good time because the Queen was traveling on the train. They had attached their own carriages and we stopped the train for them to be disconnected and shunted off to Balmoral, their Royal Scottish estate.

Canada was to be a New World to us.

We sailed from Greenock with a couple of suitcases and my large toolbox. All our belongings and about $2,000.00, which was quite a lot compared to many who were leaving. We knew at least we could fly back if necessary. Mavis recalled that our metal tea pot was tied to the handle of one of our suitcases. The ship left the dock at about 4:30 P.M. on June 12th and we said goodbye to all that was familiar. We were on deck to watch the departure. It was a damp overcast day, typical of Scotland. I had a lump in my throat leaving the old country. The Scottish Bagpipes were playing and the ship cast off.

Carole, our only child, was with us. She was three years old. Everything was going fine until the ship blew the horn which was so loud every one jumped and Carole burst out crying, scared to death. It was that which brought us down to earth, I think. It was quite cold and time to go where it was warm, so we left the deck to find our cabin. This was the first time we had been below deck. We only arrived just before sailing so we hadn't had time to do much. What a shock! The cabin was seven feet long and five feet wide with a shower at the end. It had bunk beds and the wash hand basin on the wall. For Carole, they had squeezed a small crib in the aisle. There was hardly room to breathe. No porthole, of course. I don't remember what deck it was on, but I bet it was the lowest for passenger use. If a person suffered from claustrophobia, it would have been a nightmare.

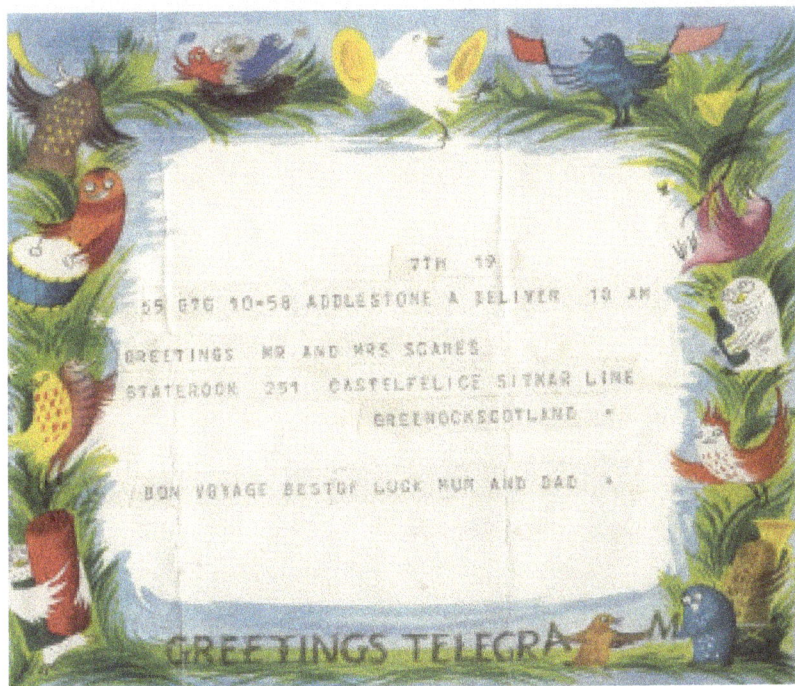

Telegram sent from Mavis' parents in 1958 to us on the Castle Felice

I was not too happy, and immediately went to the purser to see if there were any other cabins available. At first, he said no, but he must have taken pity on us because later that evening there was a message for us to go to the purser's office. There was a cabin for us on one of the upper decks with four beds and two portholes, really deluxe, near the dining room and everything else. We were so grateful!

The Atlantic in June can be quite cold and rough. We even saw icebergs. There was a very cold wind all the time until we got into the St Lawrence River. The rough seas affected a lot of the passengers, but we fared well. The stewards were good to us and took a liking to Mavis and Carole – not that Carole took a liking to them. I can remember one of them giving her some attention and all she could say was "stupid, stupid, stupid", and that didn't go down too well. Actually, they were more interested in Mavis than Carole at the time. That's for sure!

We enjoyed the cruise and the crew and passengers. We met a young woman, Una, and her son, Andy, who were going to Montreal to be with her husband, Derick. Also another couple that became friends were John Black and his wife and family, but they were not going to settle in Montreal. It was due to Una telling us about her husband's experience and with his employment we decided to stay in Montreal and not go on to Ottawa to the job at Chalk River.

We arrived in Montreal early on June 16, 1957 and were to disembark that morning. We had no plans as to where to go. Everyone was rushing around getting organized. Our luggage was on the dock for us to pick up, so finally when we were ready, we headed ashore to find it.

There was nobody there to meet us or advise us, so we decided the best thing to do was get a taxi and ask the driver take us to a place where we could find accommodations. We couldn't speak French so that was a problem. We loaded our suitcases and my toolbox into the taxi and off we went with no clue where he was going to take us. We finished up right in the center of the city in a room in a house belonging to a French lady. It was on the second floor, and the trolley wires were level with the window. It was reasonably clean so we decided it would do for a start.

We hadn't been in the room for five minutes before Carole picked up a glass of dirty water that had been used as a flower vase and drank it. It worried us, of course, being in a strange country, in case it would make her sick, but fortunately it didn't. The French lady had very limited English but we got on well with her. She took Mavis to the store and helped in every way she could. We had a stove in the room and were able to fix our meals. It was a noisy part of town on a main road. The trolley buses started very early and the neon signs kept our room light all night. It was hectic in a way compared to what we had been used to back home, but Mavis was good and accepted it.

My first job was to find employment, so the next day I headed to Canadair, a large aircraft factory, to see if I could find a job. Canadair was about ten miles from downtown Montreal, but there was good public transportation and I was able to take a tram all the way there.

I filled out an application form and was interviewed for a position. They decided they could use me as an Inspector, and gave me a start date about five days ahead, which allowed us time to get settled and look around for a more permanent place to live.

We didn't have any furniture or much in the way of cooking utensils or even dishes. We had a lot of things to organize and buy.

There was a heat wave at the time we were living in the city and the temperature was up to 94 degrees and very humid. We wanted to have the windows open but it was so noisy and dusty. It was not very pleasant. Mavis wasn't bored. It was hot for her, but she was able to fill her days while I was out job hunting and after I started my new job. We stayed down town for about two weeks until we found an apartment to rent. Not knowing much about the city and not having a vehicle or even a driving licence, it was a little difficult to find the perfect place to live. We did what worked out for the best and moved into an apartment block within sight of the Canadair plant, Tasse apartments. I didn't need a car. I could walk to work and even make it home at lunchtime if necessary. The stores were within walking distance so we were off to a good start. There was even a preschool in the apartment for Carole to attend.

Chapter 6

LIFE IN MONTREAL, CANADA, WITH THE FAMILY

Mavis, Carole and I when we first arrived in Montreal.

We bought a mattress for us and Carole, some used furniture, knives, forks, pots, pans and in no time, we were set up. There was a park nearby where Mavis could take Carole during the day and they could walk to the stores in Ville Saint Laurent. The supermarkets really opened our eyes. Back in England there was still a shortage of many things. Having all the good food and variety was something new to us.

It was a good part of the island to live. Even the apartments where we lived were not too bad. We didn't see or know of any trouble in the area. We checked the local want ads for items we needed and it wasn't long before we had all the necessities in the way of household items. We quite enjoyed ourselves going to the sales. We had kept in touch with Una and met her husband Dereck – they were a help to us. Dereck had been over for a few months and had gotten established.

Canadair was manufacturing the CL44 cargo plane, a conversion of the Bristol Britannia with a swing tail designed so the cargo could be loaded directly into the rear of the plane. They had orders for twenty-nine planes, a contract that would last about three years. It was quite a good company to work for, and the job I had was acceptable to me for a start. I think I was getting about two dollars an hour, which was good for the times, and more than I was earning in England. We were glad to stay in Montreal and not go to Ontario.

It took us some time to settle down, buy a VW, and take my driving test. When I took the test the first time, I made the mistake of driving on the wrong side of the road. I turned into a road with no other cars and automatically moved over to the left. The tester said, "You came from England, no doubt. You had better go and practice some more". The next time I took it, I drove to the test place in Montreal in a very heavy snow storm and the tester came out to the car looked at the car, the weather, and me, and said, "If you got here in this you must be able to pass the test." and that was it. He had me drive him to a store to get some groceries and take him back to the office to do the paperwork, and that was it, I had passed.

Montreal is a beautiful city with lots of places to go and things to see, so we enjoyed being there. The U.S. border was about 60 miles south. We would visit Plattsburg and Burlington and numerous other places. There were so many things we could afford compared to England. We bought a new washing machine and a colonial living room set. We were like kids in a candy store. At first, we were spending faster than I was earning. I decided it was time to get an extra job to get some more money. I got a second job in the evening in a pharmacy cleaning the floors. I didn't have to do it for long. The owner offered to have me paint his garage floor one weekend, so I went there, and while I was working his young son started giving me a hard time, so I gave him a swat across the butt. It worked. Then I started to worry until I could talk to his father the next evening. He said that's okay, he must have deserved it. That sure wouldn't happen these days.

The summers were really hot and enjoyable compared to England, but we were to learn the winters were frigidly cold. We had 120 inches of snow average each year. The city was organised with many snowploughs and trucks to remove the snow from the roads as soon as it fell. While we were living in the apartments at Ville Saint Laurent it was okay as I was able to walk to work. We lived in the apartments for two years, and while we were there Jamie was born. He arrived April 2, 1959 at Catherine Booth Hospital.

Mavis had a hard-long time in labour with him. It was tough on her. Her doctor was Doctor Linklater, who was good and looked after her well. Almost as soon as Mavis came home, Uncle Bill, Mavis' dad's brother, turned up wanting to be given attention so he wasn't really very welcome. He did visit us off and on over the years and was very generous. He brought clothes for Mavis and Carole and specialty groceries from New Jersey. I remember there was still snow on the ground in April that year.

Family trip to Niagara Falls with Carole, Mavis (taking photo)
Mavis' Uncle Bill.

Canadair was a good company. I worked in Inspection, at first checking templates and mold lofts, as they are called, which are contours at different sections of a curve where the planes were laid down full size and molds and templates were made from them for structural units. Most of the guys I worked with spoke French, but I was accepted and got on quite well. I used to walk home to lunch most days, unless the snow was too thick. I hadn't been there long before I was offered a job as a planner and I was moved to a large planning office. There was very little French spoken in the office.

I was working with a guy who helped me get started and before long I was doing as well as anyone. I did a lot of sheet metal and planning for air ducts for the heating systems on the engines. Later in the program, I finished up with the fuel system. This plane had what was called Integral Fuel Tanks, which meant the whole wing was the fuel tank. After the wing was assembled, it had to be placed in a large jig and filled with a slushing (sealing) solution, then rotated so that every area of the inside of the wing was covered with the solution so that fuel could not leak.

I had the responsibility of planning the manufacture and installing all the details that went inside the wing and making sure everything made was listed on the assembly lists, which was the installation check list. If anything was missed, and not installed before the slushing, it was a serious problem. These lists were not just common to the fuel system, but to every installation. When the aeroplane was ready to be signed off as complete, every detail had to be accounted for.

At final assembly of the first aeroplane there were a lot of raised eyebrows and people losing sleep. I was really lucky and everything was in its place, but I can't say I wasn't concerned. There was a lot of pressure. People were having heart attacks. One guy in our group on the electrical system died. I had a sore stomach and went to the doctor for a barium test to make sure I didn't have a stomach ulcer.

Finally, the first aeroplane was complete and passed inspection. The total contract was 29 aeroplanes and eventually we came to the end of the contract and lay off time came. I was offered a position with estimating, but decided I would be under a lot of pressure again and decided I would be better in a shop job at a Journeyman machinist bench. I started at that on a weekly rotating shift. I did well on the job but the rotating shifts were more than I could handle.

Rented at bottom of Olivier St. in Cartierville and later bought 12345 Olivier St. at the top of the street.

The apartments were not the best to raise the children and it was nearly time for Carole to start elementary school, so we decided to look around for a different place to live. We were lucky, and found a nice apartment in a house just up from the river, about five miles from my work. It was owned by two German brothers who lived there, Helmet and Emiel. It was a three-plex. There was one other family with one child Max, Mickey and Kathy Parker.

Montreal is on an island, and the river at the bottom of our street was La Riviere des Prairies, the back river of the island. It was about one third of a mile wide.

The City of Montreal is on the St Lawrence River where the ocean-going ships came to the big harbour. No large ships used La Riviere des Prairies. We were able to go fishing and had an old boat that I had made into a sailboat by putting a centerboard on it. I also made the sail from a long roll of brilliant coloured material someone had given me. It wasn't really suitable for sails, but the price was right, so I got to work on Mavis' sewing machine and made two sails. It was certainly conspicuous out there on the water, but it sailed well considering. We didn't swim in the river but the kids enjoyed it. It was quite clean and pleasant. Along the edge of the river there was fool's gold, iron pyrite.

We made a few friends on that street, and continued to see Una and Dereck. We really enjoyed living there. We also enjoyed the snow and cold weather even though it got down to six below zero sometimes. We kept our apartment warm with a space heater and it was always comfortable despite the snow and low temperatures. It was so much better than England. We made igloo snow houses, had a skating rink in the yard for Carole, and sometimes skated on the river. The river froze really thick on the sides and there was no fear of falling through. When it was breaking up in the spring, I saw kids floating on blocks of ice that had broken off. Not something I would want my children to do.

There was an outside city rink not far away that was always maintained while the weather was cold enough. The snow was enjoyable most of the time. After it snowed the sun would be out and the air would be crystal clear. We loved it. Mavis would put the kids out in their carriage between the snow banks in the sun. I played ice hockey for the Canadair hockey team. I spent many mornings and weekends skating on the local rink with Carole and Jamie. Sometimes we went to Mount Royal, a hilly area just out of the city where there was skating rinks and a beautiful park and other outdoor entertainment.

Shopping in the city was really good with Eaton's, Simpson's, and many other good stores. We were happy to be living in Montreal. There was a modern, rubber-wheel, underground railway that we could use to go down to the city and come up in the stores without seeing the light of day.

The city was installing sewers on the streets and had to dig a hole about twenty feet deep. I was working all night and being shaken out of bed during the day with the large diggers working outside, when I was trying to sleep.

There was another company I thought I would try: Rolls Royce of Canada. All went well. I was accepted there as an inspector. My position was Tool Inspector. My job was to do all the precision inspection on the new and reworked tooling that was used to machine, drill and assemble the parts for the jet engines. It was before calculators, so I would finish up with pages of figures each day to calculate dimensions. I was doing trigonometry, square roots, and everything the hard way, so by the time I was finished, some days I was worn out. The Chief Inspector's name was Alec Jowett, and we got on well together and he appreciated me. We kept in touch throughout years.

After about three years of Tool Inspecting, there was a job opening for a Subcontract Representative that I applied for and got. It was a good job requiring me to place work out to various small companies within the Montreal area. We had a list of companies that I would visit and check on. I got to know the company's capabilities and reliability. It wasn't long before I could get most things manufactured and completed on schedule. I would go and visit and they would take me to lunch. It was quite an enjoyable job.

After a couple of years of that I was offered a more challenging position as an Assistant Quality Engineer. I had been going to McGill University for a couple of years on an Industrial Engineering Extension course. With that degree and my previous education and experience, I was given the job. My boss was Harry Peare, a real good, capable, special person. We got on well together and really got things going. There was a big push for *Quality* and we were to do our best to make things happen.

We introduced numerous changes to improve things, and I did a Quality Audit of the total Manufacturing and Production facility. It took a long time, but I discovered many problems and rocked a lot of boats before I was finished.

The French situation, Federation Liberation de Quebec, was not a problem even though we were in a partly French area in Cartierville.

Carole went to Cartierville school, easy walking distance from the house. She had some good friends and they had French lessons everyday so they could communicate in French if they needed or wanted to. Jamie played with the local French children and was beginning to communicate with them in French quite well before we left. Mavis got a part time job at Simpson Sears while Carole and Jamie were at school. We had some wonderful camping trips into the States to Lake Champlain and Lake Ontario at various State Parks.

Wescott Beach near Watertown in New York State was a beautiful park on the East End of Lake Ontario. When we were there, there was a heavy squall that blew down trees and rolled up the tents of all the people who weren't there at the time to look after them and hold them up. We stood holding the pole and the frame and were able to survive it. After it was over, we helped people to clean up. We had an old VW at the time and used to fill it up until it was level with the seat backs and Carole would sit on top of it all. We visited Niagara Falls a couple of times and went completely around Lake Ontario. Later, I made a little trailer for the camping equipment. We camped on a site at Cornwall on the north shore of Lake Ontario. One summer we caught a really large carp. That was the summer, my dad, Richard, spent with us.

Algonquin Park near Ottawa was another place we camped. Our tent site was near a lake. The loons would make their early call. In the evening we would go to the dump and watch the big black and brown bears scavenging for food. We were told to clear the tent and area of all food each evening. The camp rangers would pick up all the garbage from the campsites so the bears would not raid them in the night. We met a guy who was a disk Jockey. He couldn't stop talking, but he was fun and Jamie and his son went fishing with him for perch. We had fresh fish for supper, and joined the family around their fire.

While we were living on Olivier Street, Cartierville, my dad and Mavis' mum visited for six weeks during the summer. It was a real

My Dad and I, Richard on one of his visits to Quebec.

Bob and Jamie, fishing for carp in 1966.

pleasure to have them. We were able to show them around and take them to New York and Niagara Falls and lots of other places. One of our favourite places to take people was Lake Champlain and Plattsburg. We were in New England in the fall, so we were able to see the beautiful colours. It looked as if every leaf had a light behind it – unbelievable! I tapped the maple trees in our back yard for maple syrup.

One outstanding vacation we had was when we visited Cape Cod and camped and fished. We now had our Chevy 11 station wagon. It was so much better than the VW for all our equipment. We camped there on a platform on a fresh water lake. I remember the camp stove catching on fire in the tent and I just managed to throw it out before it caught the whole place on fire. Jamie and/or Carole let the brake off on the car and it ran down hill and I just stopped it before it went into the water.

The large air force planes would take off from Oasis Airport to go on recognisance flights across the Atlantic looking for U-boats. They sounded as if they came in one end of the tent and went out the other. They were just above the ground when they crossed the campsite. The people from the campsite went to church on Sunday morning hoping to see the Kennedys who lived in Hyannis and went to their local church. We ate cod from the local restaurant that was freshly caught at Cape Cod. And we brought fresh corn on the cob from the side of the road. What a wonderful vacation that was.

On one of our trips to New York, we were going to visit Uncle Bill in New Jersey. We planned to stay in the Palisades State Park on the way. It was getting dark and we knew it was too late to get to the campsite, so we decided to find a place where we could spend the night. There were no other parks, and it was getting late, so we decided to stop in a quiet area behind some houses, park the car and spend the night. We had just settled down. Mavis and I were sleeping at the back with a couple of the kids and Carole up front.

All of a sudden, the car was all lit up. We looked out and were surrounded by police cars. They banged on the windows and made me get out. After a lot of fuss identifying us and checking us out, they said, "It is not safe to stay here. Follow us to the police yard and you can sleep there." We did, and finished up the night there.

We found the apartment block Bill lived in but didn't know the number, so we asked around, but could not get any satisfaction. We tried to knock on the doors of some of the apartments, but no one would answer the door, they just shouted through the door.

Finally, somehow, we did find him in the end. He took us to a local restaurant and had a meal. Then we found ourselves a motel. He lived in New Jersey directly across the river from the city of New York. It was really a pretty sight at night. Uncle Bill gave Carole her first camera, a Kodak Retinette 35mm.

On the way back to Montreal we decided to take a different route through Connecticut. We had never been through a state with so many toll roads. It seemed to charge us every few miles. Everything went well for a while. We were away from the tolls and heading home when all of a sudden, we had a police car on our tail sounding his siren and flashing his lights. I stopped to see what the problem was. He said, "You were exceeding the speed limit, and you should be careful with all your family". He wasn't too bad, never gave us a ticket, but made us follow him to the state border before we lost him.

We stayed in the house near the river for about three years. We liked the area where we lived and wanted to stay there. Then a house came available on the street, so we talked it over and decided to buy it. It was an older house, but had potential, so we brought it – 12345 Olivier Street. We fixed it to our liking and enjoyed it. It had three bedrooms, a large kitchen, and a living room and half basement. I wanted the basement larger and spent hours and a lot of effort enlarging it. It was quite a challenge getting the dirt out and then pouring the foundation. There was a large granite rock that was impossible to move. I shored it up, dug a hole under it and let it drop down until it was below the floor level. It sounds easy, but the earth was packed really tight and every shovel full was a big effort. I ended up using a noisy drill to move the dirt and rock. Our neighbour, who was bit of a grouch, didn't like the noise and stuck a running hose in the window on me. It was a difficult project. The forms broke when we poured the cement. It was never the best of basements, but we did get use out of it and it was better than not having one.

Nana Higgins, Grandad Scanes, Mavis, Bob, Carole, Jamie & Mike

I made quite a lot of wine and we could keep it cool in the basement. It wasn't long after we moved that Michael Robert Scanes was born. November 6, 1963. Like all the others he was a strong healthy baby and was a welcome addition to the family. When it snowed and after it cleared and the sun was out, Mavis would put him out in the warm sun between the snow banks the same way she did with Jamie in his baby carriage. Very British! We never had any sickness with the children or any problems with them keeping us up at night. Mavis was a good mother.

Our marital relationship during that period was reasonably good, but it would fluctuate. Mavis was lonely living in the French area and became involved with the Jehovah Witness organisation, mainly because she wanted the company of the young women who would visit her during the day while I was at work. I did not stand in her way. They seemed to be nice people and she enjoyed the activities. In the end she was baptised and would go to all their meetings. I attended a few when I felt it would help her but never really got involved.

She would go with them from door to door sometimes and was giving all she could considering she had a family to take care of. The problem was, they wanted more and more and she couldn't give any more, plus the fact they were pressuring her to get all the family involved and she knew that wasn't to be. They impressed on her that she would be the only one spared at Armageddon, and according to them it was to be in a short time. She went to a Jehovah Witness convention in New York and took Carole with her.

Finally, all the pressure from them and having to care for the family was too much for her and she had a breakdown and lost interest in everything. The Jehovah Witnesses deserted her saying she was being controlled by the devil. I had to tell them to stay away from the house. She was under the care of the Allen Memorial Hospital, one of the best psychiatric hospitals in the world. It took her a couple of months at least to recover from the most difficult period of her condition. She had to go there every day for a long time and take medication for ages before she was back living a "normal" life again. Her weight went down to below one hundred pounds and she wouldn't communicate.

It was during the winter one evening in 1964 when Mavis started hyperventilating and began to lose the use of her hands, arms and had trouble breathing. I didn't know what was the cause. It was late evening and snowing and the only thing I could do was to drive her to the hospital in the city. It was a tough drive. When we arrived, staff talked to her and kept her for the night. Carole and her friend Louise, who was spending the night, watched Mike and Jamie. Prognosis was a reaction to an antidepressant medication.

We had a lady named Mrs. Travers come in from the Red Feather / Salvation Army to take care of the children when things were at their worst. She cooked for them and did some cleaning. I also went to the Allen Memorial Hospital for therapy to help me to get through it. Carole went to England to stay with Mavis' parents for several months. I was having a physical discomfort in my throat and chest like I had received bad news and it would not go away. They gave me autogenic treatment, a form of self-hypnosis to concentrate on the area and increase the blood flow to reduce the feelings. For about a year, it was a very trying time for all of us.

As Mavis improved, I was able to get some friends from work with young English wives to visit us and develop a friendship to get her mind off our problems. After they started visiting, Mavis got some new friends. Life improved when we started doing things with them.

It seemed that was what Mavis needed to turn things around. It was much better for us from there. We would go out dancing and to parties and have some good times again. We had a number of friends on the street. Jack Patterson, a Canadian, was a good friend. He was married to a French lady, but refused to speak French even to her. His job was delivering food for Stafford's food company. He was a big strong man and was a lot of help to me. One time I was heading home from work on the airport road when it was snowing and the road was a sheet of ice under the snow. I was going fine when all of a sudden, all the traffic stopped in front of me. I was in the VW. I had two choices, hit the guy in front or head across the snow at the side of the road. I took the second and finished off the road. The VW had a flat bottom so there I was stuck. I hitched a ride home and when Jack came home from work, we took his delivery van and pulled me back on the road.

Driving in snow for four months each year was not all that bad. Everyone was familiar with it, and there were not that many more accidents. Having to shovel the driveway each morning was a chore but good exercise. I hated it when I had shovelled, and went in for a cup of tea and a warm up before I left and while I was inside, the snowplough came along and made a new large pile to be cleared again – right across the driveway!

The friends I introduced to Mavis from work were John and Connie, David and Jenny and Sylvia and Allen. Connie was Mavis' best friend and helped her the most. She was a very attractive young woman with a cultivated English accent. A real charmer. John and Allen were Engineers at Rolls Royce. David worked as a Designer. They were all go-getters, and enjoyable to be with. They really put a spark in our lives. Just what we needed at the time. Sylvia and Allen are the only couple still together and we have lost touch with them all.

One of our good family friends was Reg Farrent and his wife Vi. They lived at D'Abord de Plouffe about 20 miles from us. It was Reg who got me started on wine making. He could make wine from anything, and passed on his methods and enthusiasm to me. He worked with me in the planning office. They had a daughter named Chris, a few years older than Carole.   They lived by La Riviere de Prairie also. Reg and family also moved to the States and lived on Long Island where he worked for Grumman Aircraft and did really well for himself. He passed in 1995.

The French situation with the separatists (FLQ) was beginning to get worse in Quebec during 1965 and on. We were in Montreal when President De Gaulle visited Quebec and said, "Vive La Quebec Vive La", which was the beginning of the end. Shortly after that, there were bombs being put in letter boxes and a friend of the family who had a high position at Canadair was threatened.

Expo 67, The World's Fair, was coming up which calmed things a little. They couldn't afford trouble with that, and it would scare people away coming from other countries. It was during that period that The Boeing Aircraft Company was advertising for personnel. I was interviewed at one of the large hotels. My boss, Harry, did not want to lose me but he was enthusiastic about me having the opportunity and gave me a good reference. It was about four weeks before Boeing contacted me saying they could use me as an Industrial Engineer. That was wonderful. Just what we wanted, to be away from Quebec and the cold weather and live in a place where everyone spoke English. Also, by moving to the United States, I would get a better salary.

Boeing was willing to pay our fares, all our moving expenses. Everything we had hoped for. The next hurdle was getting our visas. We filled out the applications and had our medical exams and everything else, but there was a hold up in obtaining our visas. Finally, the visas were obtained and we had to get moving on selling the house and make some quick big decisions. We put the house on the market, but had no takers. What were we to do? There was nothing else other than for me to go ahead of the family and leave them to sell the house. The decision was made. I gave my notice at Rolls Royce.

We were sorry to leave so many old friends. It was February, and the country would be snowbound. We needed the car to go with us. Boeing was willing to pay so many cents a mile plus expenses. I checked the price of sending the car freight on the railway and found out I would be ahead to put the car on the train and pick it up in Vancouver.

We went to Expo 67, which had over 100 countries exhibiting and was really successful and well done. It was built on an island in the middle of the St Lawrence River. We went about four times and saw a lot of the exhibits. I remember going into the Russian pavilion and seeing the Sputnik, and the first manned space capsule, and a lot of other space exhibits.

The American pavilion was a geodesic dome that was very impressive. They had a good space exhibit and a yellow New York cab from what I can remember. There was a good German exhibit that was designed and built by a person who didn't have an architectural degree, and when the news media found out there was quite a big to-do about it. It wasn't taken down and turned out to be quite a success. Since Mavis wasn't working, and could get to the exhibit any day by the train from Cartierville station that was within walking distance of our house, we bought her and Carole a passport. She was able to attend whenever she wanted. Carole was old enough and went often with her friends. I know she went quite a few times and saw a few celebrities and enjoyed herself. Later, the city hosted the Olympic games on the Island.

Chapter 7

IMMIGRATION TO THE USA

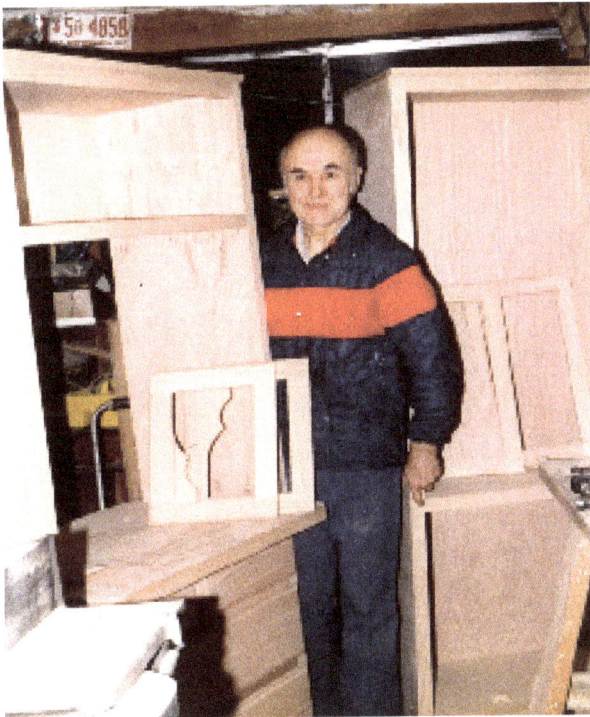

I have always enjoyed working with wood.

It was tough to leave Mavis and the children behind and get on the train alone. The train journey was four days. It was very pleasant and the meals were good. I had my own berth and met some very nice people. There was a bar where we would meet and pass time talking and playing cards. One thing that amused me was as the train moved into different provinces and the liquor laws changed the bar would open or close. The scenery was new, and seeing the Prairies and the Rockies for the first time was really wonderful. The trip was over too soon.

I made a friend of a lady who was moving to Vancouver who was an operating room nurse. When I arrived in Vancouver, there was nothing to stop me. My car was waiting for me. All the gas had been drained to transport it. I collected the car and luggage filled it with gas, bought a map and headed South. It was mid-morning on a nice day, and I really enjoyed being in a new, different place. When I got to the border at Blaine customs, I was a little concerned, but everything went well and they didn't even ask me to open my luggage. The drive into the States was enjoyable and went quickly. I arrived in Everett at about two in the afternoon the same as arriving off the boat in Canada. Not knowing where to go, I looked around for a place to eat and stay for the first night. I finished up on Broadway in the Ripvanwinkle Motel, not a very fancy place, but clean and near to everything as far as I could tell. I found a place to eat and looked around for someone to talk to. I thought I would find someone in a bar or somewhere but no one was very sociable.

After leaving the people on the train and enjoying their company I was feeling home sick again. The empty bare motel room was even worse, so I went to bed and had an early night hoping for a better day.

When I reported to Boeing the next morning, I was ready to go. I found the Boeing Employment Office and reported that I had arrived ready to start. I asked if they had any suggestions where I could stay, and from their list of accommodations, I decided to try Alderwood Manor run by a lady called Mrs Flinn. It was about ten miles from the employment office. She lived in a large split level back off the road on about five acres. She was a widow with two daughters who took in boarders. At that time, she had about ten or twelve living in the house. She was a good cook and took care of us fairly well, making our lunches and beds and she kept a clean place. It was good to have the company of all the other men who worked at Boeing, especially with a lot of them being new to the area and company.

I didn't go to work immediately as I had various things to do like registering my car and getting new plates etc. I had heard about the rain and it was true to form. I went to register the car and I saw a guy in a short plastic raincoat, which I thought was very practical and decided to buy one. My next stop was a store called Wig Wam where I found my plastic coat so I could be in fashion and dry. It has been a good coat and served its purpose, but I don't think I have seen another person in one. I still have it.

While I was staying with Mrs Flinn, it was a great opportunity to play bridge with her daughters and a couple of the other boarders. There was always something going on in the place. One weekend, everyone planned to go to the lake for the opening season of trout fishing and I was talked into going. The only snag was I hadn't been in the country long enough to get a resident licence. I was told I wouldn't be asked for it so I borrowed a rod and line and went along with everyone. I had hardly cast my line and a game warden was on to me and wanted to know where my licence was, and where I lived worked, and how long I had been in the country, and everything. He cut off my line and gave me a ticket that cost me $32, I think. That was the end of my fishing. I have never bought a licence since and decided that from then on, I never would. Any fishing I have done was in the Puget Sound before it was necessary to have a licence. What they gained up front they lost in the end. Now, as a senior, I think I can fish without a licence.

I had made a friend, Phil, among the other boarders and we went to Seattle to the Space Needle and other places together. I never went dancing or other social events. I enjoyed my new job at Boeing and that kept me busy along with overtime. Also, as I mentioned there was always some activity at the lodging. While I was away from Mavis, I was able to call her at least once a week on a special line account belonging to Boeing, so we were always in touch.

Finally, Mavis couldn't wait any longer to sell the house. I think at first it was a novelty being alone and she enjoyed it. I had left a cellar full of wine at the house, so she could have the odd party. She was a good friend with the real estate lady, and things went well for a while. But she started to get the wrong type of attention from a neighbour that upset her. Due to the French separatist problem (Federation Liberation de Quebec) there was a mass evacuation of Quebec by the English-speaking population, and property wasn't selling very easily.

The house had been on the market for six months and the family visas were going to expire so it was time to leave the house and Montreal in the hands of the real estate agent. It hadn't been all bad for Mavis as our friends kept her busy while she was alone. The family finally flew out on air France and arrived here happy and ready to start their new life. The fashions in Montreal when they left were ahead of Seattle and they were wearing what then was called the new look – very short skirts. When Mavis and Carole got off the plane, their short skirts received a lot of attention.

It was good to see them all again and to be able to tell them all my news and show them around what little I had been shown. Before they arrived, I had found a house in south Everett on Jordan road or 100th that we could move into. It belonged to a military person who was out of town. It was everything we needed to get started including being near my work.

Our furniture was being shipped so we were without for about a week. I bought a double mattress and we borrowed plates, dishes, and a kettle from a neighbour to tide us over. Finally, everything arrived and we were settled. We got Carole into Cascade High School and Jamie into Evergreen Middle School. Carole was a year ahead, so it was an easy time for her. Her French was years ahead. They hadn't even started French at her grade here, so she finished up assisting the teacher. Things went well for her in high school with good marks and popularity. She was Homecoming Queen her senior year. I remember how she handled it without concern. She had to stand up in the stadium and give a little speech and she didn't even write anything down on what she was going to say.

Jamie struggled with reading and had to try really hard to make his grades. We did all we could to assist him by asking for special classes and offering him help at home but he still struggled. He has a good mechanical head and enjoys working on cars.

Michael we got into kindergarten a year early, and he wasn't ready for it, so he was held there for an extra year. From then on there was nothing holding him. He had the ability to go as far as he wanted. He graduated from Cascade High School and joined the Air force. We were all here and settled down to life in the USA.

Chapter 8

WORKING FOR BOEING

Bob received many Time Study awards working at Boeing in Industrial Engineering. Shaking hands with supervisor, Mr. Clancy

When I was interviewed in the hotel in Montreal, the person who interviewed me was Paul Gosney. He was an Industrial Engineering supervisor. He had interviewed me to work for him, so he was the first supervisor I reported to. At that time he was loading the machine shop, which means insuring they had enough work, manpower and equipment. I was familiar with a lot of the machines and had no problem fitting in.

I hadn't been there long before the first 747s were rolled out. It was quite a HUGE show. I think the first aeroplane was sold for $21,000,000 and now they are about $190,000,000. They had quite a number of customers on the firing order, and it looked as if we had a job for life. (Note: The last 747 rolled out Dec. 2022).

Our machine shop was used mainly for emergent part shortages and specially made parts to fit a certain aircraft requirement. When an aeroplane was not as per drawings, and a special part had to be made to fit, Blue Streak had to make it. We had a good machine shop with good capability.

We also looked after the assembly and plastic shops. I was involved in doing methods studies, new equipment justification, manpower forecasting, and the long-range forecasting. During the method studies, I would calculate potential cost savings and was responsible for many large suggestions that resulted in big savings. I became good at turning processing changes and new equipment into savings. If a supervisor required a new machine, I could develop a cost saving on the number of parts that would be manufactured on it and how much saving a part could be accumulated in a year. With my machine shop and sheet metal background it all came easy for me.

After being in the machine shop for about two years I was transferred to the Interior Shop where they made and finished all the interior panels for the aircraft including side walls, ceiling panels and all the interior finishing. The side walls had to have decorative designs on them per the requirements of the buyer. Panels were made with a honeycomb core called Nomex with a fibre glass cover and a Mylar decorated sheet on the surface. The Mylar covering had to go through a silkscreen printing machine to have the design requested by the customer.

One thing I justified in the silk screen shop was a colour analyser at $60,000, which was quite a lot of money at that time. I developed a load plan for laying up the side walls on the big moulds. We did a memo motion study on the large ovens that all the lay ups were cured in. It involved a movie camera to be set up taking a frame every twenty seconds. The result when run at normal speed would show the total oven operation for a day in less than hour. After working in Interiors for about a year, the big lay off occurred and the company manpower dropped from 110,000 manpower to 40,000.

I was one of the people laid off.

We had a large mortgage on the new house we had bought, but we didn't have an excessive payment. Mavis had a job with Sears in the

96

catalogue department, so it could have been worse. At first, we thought it would be a problem, but I went around all the local companies and filled out applications and interviewed. In no time I was working at Boat Land USA on the docks. It was interesting work and I enjoyed working with my hands again. I started working with a young man who didn't think I would be able to do the job, but it wasn't long before I earned his respect and we got on really well.

We had to do fibre glass repairs when boats hit logs and had been damaged in other ways. We installed electrical equipment and adapted trailers to boats and wire lights. We took new boats out and tried out the engines with different pitch propellers and everything else necessary to complete or repair a boat. I didn't do engine repairs. They had a separate shop for that. I made some good friends and enjoyed my time there.

Unfortunately, that didn't last forever since the store closed down and moved to Bellevue. That put me on the street again. It wasn't long before I had a job installing gutters for a company – quite a job. I was sent out with an experienced installer and it wasn't long before I was making myself useful.

They were all young men and one morning we were on a job in Edmonds on a new, two-story house. The roof wasn't finished and it was wet and had pine needles on it. The guys were standing on the edge of the roof leaning over and putting in gutter spikes and it was something I didn't feel safe doing. When I went back to the office, I told them I was sorry but I didn't feel safe under those circumstances. The company was run by a couple of young guys who used to work for a company called Everett City Heating, so they were understanding, and said they knew someone who they thought could use me. I went for an interview and the next day I was working again. They had a fleet of GMC trucks that had to be maintained, and I was to look after them and do odd jobs around the company. I finished up installing in three phases, wiring new machines, doing sheet metal work, and many other jobs. I got on really well. We each received a turkey at Christmas. They allowed me to go to their property and pick up a load of cut wood in one of the company trucks. They were really good to me. The manager said he would train me as a refrigeration serviceman, but I received a letter from Boeing asking me to return to them. It was a difficult decision and I didn't like letting Everett City Heating down, but there was no doubt that returning to Boeing was the most secure move to make. I was sorry to leave Everett City Heating.

I returned to Boeing at plant two in Seattle on Marginal Way, thirty-three miles to drive each way. It made a longer day for sure.

The job I had when I returned was to make a load plan for two-part makers. They were numerically controlled, five axis machines that produced parts from aluminium extrusion at extremely high speeds. Also included were three Sundstrand Milling machines and large numerical mills. It was a full-time job to keep them loaded, and I had a big job collecting all the data.

We had a really good general supervisor who worked with us and really took care of us. On a Friday he would take us to lunch to Ivars Salmon House or another good place. I really did well there and was liked and had a job that offered a lot of potential. The only thing that was spoiling it was the travelling distance. I had a couple of riders for a while, but that didn't make the distance any shorter. I was driving an old dodge truck with a slant six engine. The speed limit at that time was 70mph, and I would do 70 plus all the way.

One evening I looked at my tires and there was a large blister on one of my front tires. The rubber had parted from the inner fabric and had blown up. I was really lucky it never blew at 70 mph. I had to get really tough with one of the lady passengers to put on her seatbelt. She would sit there and go to sleep and if I had been in an accident, she would have been right through the wind shield. I was really strict on time and would not wait more than five minutes beyond the agreed pick-up time. A couple of times I had to leave my ride behind.

One afternoon I left work at three and ran out of gas as I was going through the tunnel under the convention center. I just managed to coast all the way through and stop at the vee at the end of the on-ramp. I waited there from 3:15 until 6:00 P.M. to get help. Police went past a couple of times, but never came back. Then finally a private car stopped and took me to the university district to get some gas. What a night!

While I was working in plant 2, I watched for openings in the Everett plant. Finally, after having been at plant 2 about a year, there was an opening with one of my old supervisors from when I worked there before. The opening was in the wire shop and my supervisor was a German guy called Marty. I was estimating and loading the wire bundle assemblies and taking care of bar charts. There are at least a thousand different bundles in a plane, and every plane is different in some way due to the customer requirements. I had the responsibility of estimating thousands of wire bundles with another Industrial Engineer. We developed a form that covered every different item on all the different bundles, and we did time studies to establish the time required doing each operation. Eventually, we managed to get it down to a repetitive operation. From the estimates, bar charts had to be made for the employees who built the bundles to work from. It was quite a job. A complicated job that got a bit old with time. I finished up writing the logic for a computer program to simplify it. They were writing the program when I left for my next assignment.

While I was working at the wire shop, I was selected to go to British Aircraft in Weybridge, England to work on the manufacture of the 767-strut program. I worked with the two English planners that were sent to Boeing for the preparation of the work. I was within days of the family flying out. Then out of the blue they cancelled the requirement for Industrial Engineering on the program. I had made a lot of preparation like selling my truck and renting my house and everything necessary. We were to move into the Holiday Inn for a week before going. That was a major turning point in my life in many ways. If we had gone to England, Mavis and I may never have divorced.

From there I was transferred to another new program, taking care of the manufacture of the on-board loader. We were manufacturing four 747s with an open nose so freight could be loaded in the front of the aeroplanes. This was alright, but Saudi Arabia would not buy them unless they had a means of raising the cargo up to the level required, so the onboard loader was built to carry in the aeroplane and when it landed the loader was required to come out the front and unfold its four legs and the platform was there to be raised and lowered for unloading the cargo. It was mentioned later that it was doubtful that it was ever used to any extent. I saw a demonstration and I am not surprised.

From that assignment I was moved to the tube shop to develop a load plan. This was required because the tubing was manufactured

Working at Boatland USA during Boeing Layoff. Carole, my daughter is on the right.

Boeing is the reason Bob and his family moved to Everett, WA. USA in 1968.

with various materials, diameters, and wall thicknesses. There was also a variation of the bend radius, angle of bend, and rotation. To manufacture each tube, a numerically controlled program was developed for a specified bending machine.

The most time required to produce a tube is the mechanical set up of the bending machine. The load plan was to look ahead for a month and sort all the tubes by material diameter wall thickness and bend radius. Also assigning tubes to a particular machine so each machine only had to be set up once for a month supply of required tubes of similar characteristics. This load plan was very successful, and during the four years I was there the tube shop ran very well.

While I was working in the tube shop, Carole was hired by Boeing. We worked together for a short time in the same department until Carole was transferred to Interiors. She worked at Boeing for 5 years before going into teaching high school.

My next assignment was back with the machine shop and sheet metal area. The machine shop general supervisor was Mr. Maury Kline. I did well there and was regarded with a lot respect by supervision. They gave me credit and respect for my background knowledge and experience compared to the young college guys who were recently employed.

During most of my time with Boeing I enjoyed my work. I had good relations with supervision and was a lead a couple of times. I never had any ambition to be in a supervisory position. The amount of financial benefit was not worth the worry of being responsible for others work. I didn't do any more overtime than necessary. When I walked out the door each afternoon, I wanted to leave the work behind. Most times I did.

I have no regrets that I worked there, but I was happy to retire when I reached my 65th birthday.

Chapter 9

DIVORCE AND PWP

Bob & Nita Ballroom Dancing

Mavis and I were married on Sept 6, 1952 and we anticipated a marriage for life; neither my parents nor Mavis' were divorced. For many years, our married life was enjoyable and seemed to be working well from my point of view. Life went quite well for a long while, and we seemed to enjoy each other. In many ways there wasn't ever a lot of affection demonstrated between us or within the family compared to some other families. Neither of our own families showed very much between each other.

In 1963 Mavis had a nervous breakdown. From then until we separated our relationship, she would go up and down. We worked well together with the children, and were always agreeable with any discipline. We didn't have mood swings, but there was not a lot of affection between us when we were alone. I am a firm believer in the saying. "Men give love for sex and women give sex for love". So, once things started going downhill, the problems compounded themselves until things fell apart. I know that some of the therapy and counseling Mavis received at the Allen Memorial Hospital was negative in respect to our marital relationship. The analyst put me down a lot saying I was a partial cause of her breakdown. I feel that this was the beginning of the end for us.

Just before our twenty-fifth anniversary I was away in England visiting my father because he was sick, and came home to find Mavis had found another man. She told me she wanted to leave and said, "I cannot live without him."

It came as quite a shock. I knew she had been going out to parties with the people where she worked and when I offered to go she didn't want me there. I know I could dance as well as any of them, but I didn't think it was as serious as it turned out to be. I was at a loss for words and pleaded with her to no avail.

His name was Jake and he worked at Cable TV with her. He was just twenty-seven years old. Mavis was forty-three. It was no doubt that during one of the down swings in our relationship he must have given her the right attention – when she was most vulnerable and needy.

It was a real shame because we had everything going for us in so many ways. No doubt we needed some marriage counseling. I shouldn't have let things get to the state they had. It came at a very bad time. Mavis' mother and sister were due to arrive for a months' vacation in two weeks from when she told me. Mavis said, "If you don't tell them perhaps by the time they go I will feel differently".

We spent two weeks on the Oregon coast with that hanging over us trying to be normal. It was very difficult and they sensed there were problems and assumed I was the cause. They thought I was upset with them being there.

After we came back from the coast and were still on vacation, Mavis was making excuses to go to the mall but she was taking off to meet Jake.

We finally took Jean and Mavis' mum to the Vancouver airport and saw them off. They still didn't know she planned to leave me. When we came home, she still wanted to leave, so I helped her load the truck and off she went with as much of her belongings as it was practical for her to take to the apartment she rented. I was left with the children. Carole was living in Bellingham and going to Western Washington University, and Jamie and Michael were in high school. Both Jamie and Michael were upset at the time and Jamie wanted to damage Jake's Corvette, but I told him it would do no good and convinced him to change his mind.

Just a couple of weeks before, Carole had said to Mavis, "All my friends' parents are getting divorced, its good you and dad get on so well." Once the boys found it would not interfere with their lives too much, they settled down to the idea and just accepted things. I was a good cook and was able to take care of our meals. As it was, for a while before she left, Mavis had been letting them fend for themselves more and more. When I had the full responsibility of the kitchen, they were better off in some ways.

I laid down the law in the house and made them take care of their bedrooms and wash their dishes and not leave them in the sink. We had our ups and downs but it wasn't long before things were running smoothly and we had a good bachelor pad. Once I noticed Jamie was giving the greenhouse a lot of attention and when I went in there, I found a good healthy marijuana crop. When he came home that evening I said, "You know, if the police come here and find that, you won't be living here for long. You will have to live with your mother or in a foster home". It was gone the next day.

Things went well as far as I can remember so there couldn't have been anything serious. Michael had been closer to his mother than me, so it was quite hard on him. When Mavis left, she said she would take him when she got settled. I did not put any pressure on him either way, but let him come to me over a period of time and it was not too long before we got along well together. Both the boys were fairly independent. I continued at work and everything went well there. I didn't put Mavis down to the boys, just told them that we had grown apart and it was happening with lots of ladies at this time in their lives. Some mothers left when they thought the children were old enough to take care of themselves. They saw how hurt and lost I was. By the time Mavis was able to take him it would have been another disruption in his life that was not favorable so he stayed with me.

We were divorced on Nov 18, 1975, 25 years and 2 months.

After a few months of feeling sorry for myself I found an organization called "Parents Without Partners" (PWP) and joined. PWP became everything to me. It gave me the company I seriously needed. We didn't have any friends during our marriage that I could turn to. With PWP I was able to attend so many things: discussion groups, meetings, dances and other activities. After a while I became the programs Education Director. My main function was to organize and lead discussion. The topics of the discussions covered everything from children to anything related to marriage: dating, sexuality, relationships, everything and anything.

I would study the topics I was going to lead a discussion on and be more than prepared. It was a method of analysis for me, because I had an opportunity to discuss all my thoughts and fears and anything I had or did in my life that I wanted to resolve with a group. I did this for a great number of discussions and subjects. I later became Vice President then eventually President.

We made our money mainly from our dances for the children's activities and our biggest expense was the disc jockey for the music. When I became President, I arranged for us to buy our own tape deck amplifier and speakers so we could supply our own music. I took the job as disc jockey and my friend, Maurice, would help me. Our chapter of PWP was richer than it had ever been before. We needed extra folding tables at the hall. Previously, we had rented them. We became financially able to purchase the 21 extra oak tables.

It was not beyond possibility that we could have invested in a building of our own if things had continued to progress. It was not easy to get the kind of help and support to run the chapter. The more a person did the more they expected that person to do. Eventually, I was loaded down beyond it being a pleasure anymore, and gave the whole thing up. This was after seven years of member ship.

I never went steady with anyone for the first couple of years while I was still hurting from the loss of my wife. Then finally I had some steady girlfriends. I usually stayed with them at least a couple of years. We saw many ladies come and go in the PWP group and we had guys who would take advantage of their vulnerability. Usually the ladies were recently from a broken marriage, lonely and clutching for any offer of kindness or attention they could get. I advised them at our new members meeting to talk to the old-time members in the group about any guy who made advances to them. I even wrote a handout to give to new lady members.

It was tough for them, and I know a number of them got hurt because the guys who went after them knew how they reacted and went with them until they got fed up, then moved to another woman leaving them embarrassed and hurting. Sometimes they would leave PWP. We wouldn't see them again. But there were a lot of people we helped in many ways. As a leader of the PWP, I was in a position to meet and get involved with quite a few ladies, but I tried to set an example by staying in relationships for a year or more. There is no doubt leaving a relationship or being left after a long period is more likely to hurt. I hurt a couple of ladies and was really hurt once myself. The old saying, "It's better to have loved and lost than never loved at all". It is true but it can really hurt.

The sad thing is, a lot of people cannot let their feelings go. After the first couple of let downs, people start setting up a barrier and will not let themselves get deeply involved and in love again. I think I have that problem. I have never exposed myself again and made myself vulnerable to suffer through the loss again. I have seen so many marriages start with enthusiasm and fall apart in no time. It's hard to know what a good mix or combination is. Some of the most unlikely couples make it when the ones with everything going for them fail. One PWP marriage lasted three days.

Bob & Alice at his house in Everett at Christmas

Chapter 10

SEATTLE MOUNTAINEERS

After divorce I was very active in the Mountaineers, teaching XC skiing at Stampede Pass

Another organization that has been a big help to me during my single life has been the Seattle Mountaineers. I joined to take advantage of the hikes and backpacking trips they organize. I was a member for about fifteen years.

Apart from back-packing, climbing, and dancing, I have done Nordic and downhill skiing and spent many weekends at the lodges. One hiking trip I did was for ten days with a lady called Marlene. I was packing forty-three pounds and she had twenty-seven.

I knew we were going to have a leisurely trip because she had been a smoker and couldn't go all that fast. This back-packing trip was in the Olympic National Park as shown in 102 hikes #90 Grand Valley. We started by driving to Hurricane Ridge, then turned off just before the lodge to drive along a narrow scenic dirt road.

The weather was perfect and we were hoping it would stay that way. There was a drop off at the road side of a couple of thousand feet, but the road was quite good and we didn't meet any oncoming vehicles. We continued to the end of the road to Obstruction Peak, the place our car would remain while we were on the trip.

From then on for the next ten days, we would be living out of our packs and there was nowhere to buy anything so we checked that we had all we needed. Actually, it was too late then but it was nice to know what we had. The hike started along the crest of the mountain so we could look down both sides at the beautiful views. This continued for about three miles until we reached a small peak at 6,450ft. From there we started on the steep winding track down. It wasn't long before we were in a beautiful meadow of lush flowers. We had taken flower books and our cameras and each time we saw a different flower we would identify it from the books and from then on, we would repeat the names as we saw them again to help us remember.

We had no definite destination for the first night, so we could stop whenever we found the ideal place. The day was moving along and we needed to eat, so we decided to start looking. It was not long before we found a beautiful shady place in the long grass in the corner of a meadow covered with wild flowers. The sun was still out so we lit the Peak One camp stove and while the kettle was boiling, I set up the tent. I had brought the Jansport tent, a really good quality two-person tent, so we were going to be very comfortable. Due to the length of time we would be away and the weight we had a lot of freeze-dried food, but to start we had a small amount of perishable food so we were able have a regular dinner the first couple of nights.

I had brought a small, portable Scrabble game, so we were able to play Scrabble for an hour – something we both enjoyed. It was so peaceful and quiet and such a pleasant evening. Finally, we settled down at the end of a perfect day. We snuggled together and enjoyed a good night's sleep. The next morning, we rose leisurely, had breakfast and did all that was necessary prior to leaving this lovely spot. We still had quite a lot of elevation to lose to get to Grand Valley and the lakes we were heading for, so we continued down the rocky slopes through the open forests seeing an occasional view of the Elwha River and the forests to Mount Olympus.

We had no time-pressure or destination to make, so we just enjoyed the fresh mountain air, scenery, wild flowers, nature and each other's company. The days drifted by. We had not seen a soul for two days. Sometimes we would hear a marmot whistle and I would whistle back. We had seen a few deer and evidence of bear. It was just perfect in so many ways. We spent another night as beautiful an area as the night before. We knew that the next day we would be at Grand Lake, a place we intended to settle for a few days and go on day hikes. With that in mind, we were up and on the trail fairly early again enjoying beautiful weather except for the early morning mist, common to the mountains in the early morning. We were warm and comfortable in the tent, so sometimes we would just wait until the sun came up and the mist had cleared.

That evening we arrived at Grand Lake and found a perfect tent site not too far from the lake. We took pictures and enjoyed the view, looked at the map and talked about our plans for the following day. We decided it was time for a rest to sit around and keep within site of the tent. I had brought fly fishing gear and I knew there were trout in the lake and stream, so that was one of our goals – to catch our dinner.

We could see the fish swimming around in the clear water, but they just didn't want to take the fly or bait. It must have been the time of day, so I finally gave up and decided to try later. About five in the evening when it was calm and clear on the lake, I tried again with a different fly and couldn't go wrong. Every time I cast they would bite at the fly. I had chosen the right one for the right time. We didn't catch more than we needed, just enough for a fresh trout supper cooked on an open fire. Definitely a meal I will always remember. Next morning there were a lot of deer around which we chased off. We didn't want them nosing around the tent. We were planning to do a day hike to a peak that seemed quite near and didn't want to come back to a flattened tent. As the sun came up and it got warmer, the deer disappeared, so we were able to have our day hike without worrying.

We stayed in that area for a few days as it was so beautiful. Then we decided to move on to Moose Lake, the smaller of the two lakes in the valley which was another mile away. It was good to be up and on the trail again, even though it wasn't very far. We arrived at the next lake at about noon and found another pleasant campsite. The fishing wasn't as good there but we did catch a few.

The days were slipping by, so we decided we would plan our route back and move in that direction the next morning. The weather had been really good to us. We had no problem with bears or other wildlife. Our food was lasting well. We had been boiling our water each evening. The fuel was lasting well because we had a small fire each evening. To boil the water, we used a Crisco can that I kept the Peak One stove in.

The next few days heading back to the trail head continued to go well. The different route back took us through some beautiful old growth forest with some of the largest trees I have ever seen. We camped one night on the thick pine needles and woke up to the smell of the forest. It was beautiful. One evening we camped in a meadow just covered with Lupines and Indian Paint Brush. The grass and flowers were swaying in the breeze with the tent and the mountain in the background. It was perfect.

We had two more days and we were climbing out now to get back to Observation Peak at 6,200 ft. We had passed through Badger Valley and had seen many marmots and other wildlife and had perfect weather. The mountain hike I had dreamed about had gone beyond my expectations.

The last day was really up hill on the rock and shale mountain trail. Marlene was holding up well. It was fortunate that our packs were getting lighter without the food we had been enjoying.

We arrived back at the car happy, relaxed, and ready for a nice sit down and steady ride home. It was the end of ten days of pleasant memories and relaxation. This was typical of many backpacking trips. There were some disasters due to bad weather, but even those were fun when I look back on them.

I learned a lot from the Seattle Mountaineers courses. Scrambling is mountain climbing on the easier side of the mountain without ropes and all the other equipment that goes with technical climbing. The only climbing aid we took for the course was an ice axe. To pass the course we had to have our Mountaineering First Aid Certification, study hard, and pass the classes on back country navigation and mountain travels. We had to know how to ice axe arrest, teaching a person how to stop if they were sliding on a snow bank or glacier.

We learned to snow camp to survive with or without a tent in cold conditions. We had to climb to the top of five mountains that were designated. Our Graduation Mountain was Cowboy Mountain, the highest point at Stevens Pass Ski area. The skiing season was over, so we had the place to ourselves. There were six of us left in the course. We arrived at the pass about 11:00 A.M. with our tents, X-country skis, and all that was necessary to stay overnight.

After stowing our gear and eating a snack, we were given lessons on ice axe arrest. A steep hill had been selected that a person would slide down out of control. We had to start sliding on our backs then roll over on our stomachs with ice axe held in both hands digging the point of the axe in to stop our descent. We did that for a couple of hours before we all were proficient. The next was trepanning – sliding down on your butt using the ice axe as a brake. It was a good easy way down a fairly steep slope with the ability to keep control of your speed.

We then started to prepare for our night's camp. I had been selected to sleep in the tent. Two were to sleep in a snow house and two in a snow cave that we all had to help them build.   For the ice house we cut square blocks of snow and built an igloo making the top of the entrance below the two sleeping platforms so the heat would be at the top where the people were going to sleep. The ice cave we dug into a bank of deep snow and did the same thing keeping the entrance low. By the time we were finished we were ready to eat.

We skied around a little until it was nearly dark and time for bed. I spent the night in the tent. I had a minus six below sleeping bag and slept on a Beauty Rest inflatable air pad. Except for being thirsty during the night I had a good night. When I was thirsty, I decided to put my hand out of the tent door and get a handful of snow, but when I did it was frozen solid so I went without my drink.

Next morning after breakfast we went on our last climb to the top of Cowboy Mountain. It was quite a climb. The snow was firm on the ski slopes, so we went most of the way on that, then scrambled up the rest

Bob taught skiing for the Mountaineers at Stampede Pass.
He also helped with wiring and repairs in Meany Lodge. He spent many weekends
there teaching, dancing and skiing. Here he is XC skiing with his daughter, Carole.

in the soft snow until we were at the top. It was much higher than the ski lifts go. It was a beautiful view. Coming down we could trepan or walk, whichever was easiest. When we got back to the tent we put on our skis and spent a couple of hours practising telemarking to round off the weekend. We had already spent a day in the woods practising our navigating skills and had an evening on avalanche training.

I took and passed the Telemark course at Mount Baker. Telemarking is downhill skiing on X-country skis. Meany Lodge was my favourite lodge and that was where I taught X-country skiing for seven years. We would start our teaching on the first weekend after New Year, and continue until March 1st. Usually, I had about eight to ten people of varying ages in my classes at the intermediate skiing level. By the time I had finished with them, they were doing quite well on their downhill techniques and started some telemarking and parallel turns on their X-country skis. I had some good classes and helped a lot of people.

I completed all the levels of folk dancing classes the Mountaineers offered and enjoyed it. We would often have a band at the lodge on a weekend, so we could folk dance on the Saturday of our skiing weekends.

New Year's Eve was always a good evening to spend at Meany Lodge. The lodge is about three miles off the road near Stampede Pass and could sleep about 150 people at a push. There were three rope tows. People who have X-country skis could ski in or tow in behind the snow cat on a long rope with loops. The Cat held about twenty-two sitting. Usually, beginners and children preferred to ride, then everyone who skied towed. Sometimes we had up to eighty on tow. It was a fun way to start or finish the weekend.

The best was when everyone was in the lodge on New Year's Eve and had a great dinner after a good day skiing. After dinner we danced until about 11.45 P.M. Then everyone went to the bottom slopes where we had a bonfire. Then just before midnight, a line of skiers started at the top and wove their way down the slopes with a red flare held high in the air and arrived at the bottom at midnight. A volley of fireworks was set off and everyone held hands around the fire and sang Auld Lang Syne. It was quite an exciting way to bring in the New Year. I have done it many times.

I wish it were possible for me to do again. The lodge is all wood and was built in 1928. Drinking or smoking are not allowed in the lodge but the good company makes up for it – it isn't missed. There is a sign that says anyone found smoking will be treated like a fire and will have a bucket of water thrown on them.

During my membership with the lodge, I learned to cross country ski and downhill ski and I really enjoyed it. The people that attend are really special, and I have made many friends who have given me their emotional support since my accident. I have been on many long X-country trips and taught X-country skiing and wouldn't change a minute of it. Another popular pastime in the lodge during the evenings was playing bridge – just one more thing I really enjoyed.

Chapter 11

SINGLE LIFE

Square dancing with Alice

My ballroom dancing started in England when I was sixteen. I got to Bronze medal level. I continued to ballroom dance throughout my life taking many classes after my divorce and becoming quite proficient in most dances including Latin dancing the Cha Cha, Rumba, Tango, Mambo and others. I completed Square Dancing lessons to Main Stream level. I danced with the Single Stars Square dance club and went to many state dance festivals until I had had enough of it. Then I started full-time Round Dancing.

Round dancing is ballroom dancing with a caller. I was dancing with Alice as a partner for about five years until we were at the advanced level and quite good. We would try most dances even if we hadn't even been taught the steps. Alice had learnt to ballroom dance with me so well that she was able follow my lead right or wrong, and so long as we did not disrupt the floor, we fitted in and it was accepted that we knew the dance.

Alice and I went together for five years and spent quite a lot of time on my motorcycle and traveling. I taught her to X-country ski and she often came to Meany Lodge. My daughter, Carole, and her husband, Scott, also came to ski and spend a couple of weekends at Meany. Alice and I collected Elderberries and Black berries and made wine most years. Now she makes it for herself each year. We got along fine most of the time. We met square dancing at the Single Stars, a Square and Round dance club. Our main interest was dancing most of the time we were together. I taught her to ballroom until she was doing so well that we took lessons together. With round dancing we learnt together and with that you have never finished lessons. We would go to weekend dance seminars and really have a wonderful time together. We also had a lesson at least once a week and really enjoyed it.

We did many things together: hiking, camping, cooking, and skiing. When we went to a seminar and there was a new style square dress on display, I would sketch the dress that Alice liked and she would make it for herself. She was always getting compliments on her dresses. She is a great seamstress and made them so well.

We went on a couple of vacations together. One was a three-thousand-mile drive, camping most nights. We left Everett with all our camping gear in Alice's Nissan Stanza and drove south all the way to the Grand Canyon, stopping and camping each night at various sites. The weather was perfect and we shared the driving and enjoyed each other's company very much.

The Grand Canyon was beautiful, unbelievably big and worth seeing. We spent a couple of days there then went to Bryce Canyon. It was just as beautiful and shouldn't be missed. We camped each night and woke up some mornings with ice on the windows of the car. Fortunately, we had a good double sleeping bag and were warm. The last state park we visited was Zion National Park. It is necessary to see it to appreciate the whole geographical formation of the area.

We also spent about three days in Las Vegas and had a wonderful time playing the slots, swimming at the motel, taking photographs and shopping. Two wonderful weeks I wouldn't have missed for anything, and I look back on the trip as one of the best vacations I can remember. We got on really well for that whole two weeks together and except for one small misunderstanding that led to words it went perfectly.

During the time we were together I helped Alice through a number of hard times with her kids, house and work situation. We got on well together most of the time, but if I upset her, she would take quite a while to get over it. Whereas I can row on the dance floor and forget it by the time we sit down.

Towards the end of our time together, Alice would get really upset if I mentioned a thing about how to do a step or her dancing and it would frequently spoil the evening. I told her a number of times it couldn't go on. I could not take it. Finally, we were at a round dance class one Wednesday evening at Haller Lake and she became really upset when we were learning a Tango and I said, "I think it goes like this". She embarrassed me so much I said, "Its over Alice," and walked out and went home. She had her car there so was able to get home. After that I would not continue our relationship. I know she was upset, but I knew we could not have a permanent forever relationship. We parted after five really good years.

After we broke up we rarely even saw each other except the odd time at the Sons of Norway. We both went our way. Since I had the accident, we have made contact again and Alice has been a great help to me in many ways. She wrote to me with her interpretation of what she thought were the reasons for our break up, and I answered her with the following long letter and her answer.

Daughter's Note: Not sure what happened to the letters.

When Mavis left me she said "It could work out better for all of us". Of course we will never know how it would have been if we had stayed together, only what happened apart. I can't really complain as I met a lot of wonderful ladies, traveled more than I would have ever done, and I think accumulated more financially. I also had a lot more experiences like skiing, which I may not have done married. I had plenty of company when I wanted it. My work was not affected. I had the pleasure of living with the boys during their teens. We did well together and I do look back on it with a lot of pleasure and good memories.

Of my relationships as I look back, I had a lot of good times. I think the one that hurt worst was when Marlene left me after us going together for over two years. We really got on well and enjoyed many good times, but I was not ready to settle down with anyone. The boys did not seem ready to accept her. She was looking for something permanent.

It was a time when my Dad was really sick and I needed to go to England to him. He was 86 years old. Marlene and I were eating out together and she said to me, "What would you say if I said let's get married or else". I didn't take her seriously and would not give her an answer. I was not looking for marriage and I just let it go. She was in earnest and determined to marry someone else if not me. A couple of days later I had a phone call saying I had better come and see my Dad.

I immediately bought a ticket and set off to England. It was a tough time. Bob and Maureen Amato met me at the airport and we rushed directly to the hospital. It was a terrible shock to see him so frail and in a coma. I sat by him for quite a long time talking to him and holding his hand, but he never opened his eyes.

In the end I went into the nurse and sat with her and broke down. I had been up for nineteen hours and I was worn out. She gave me a cup of tea and we talked and I felt better. I went in again to him for a while, then Bob came in with the nurse and said we had better go home. We left and I was never to see him alive again. He must have been waiting for me to be there as he passed away peacefully in the night. I felt I had lost a good friend and a father. He had visited us a number of times in Canada and U.S. and we really got to know each other.

Carole was not able to get on the plane I was on. It was full, so unfortunately she never saw him again as she arrived the day after he passed on standby. Carole and I stayed in England at Maureen and Bob's house for about two weeks. I was happy to have Carole there for support. I informed all the family and friends and we had quite a turnout. The ceremony was in Addlestone Church on Marsh Lane and Dad was buried with my mother. It was a sad day for me because I had not attended my mother's funeral and it hurt to think that. It was good to see all the family and a good opportunity for Carole to meet them. I was able to get all the legal papers resolved, do some visiting, and the two weeks were soon over and we returned to the U.S.

When I returned and went to visit Marlene, I was told she had been visiting a guy she knew who was in the hospital having surgery on his leg, and they had plans to date. It was getting close to Christmas and we had plans for me to go to her place for Christmas day. I got there to spend the day to learn that she had decided to leave me for the other guy. He had bought her two dozen roses and that had clinched it. I was at a loss that day. I did find some friends in PWP to visit, but I was really hurting. It seemed it was not good to go away because when I returned, I lost my partner.

I was really disturbed by the loss of my father and Marlene at the same time. I was hurting to the extent I went to Group Health for therapy. I had a couple of visits with a counselor. He gave me medication to help me over a rough period. They said it was the double loss that was the cause of my depression. First Mavis then Marlene. Marlene married the guy within six months and was divorced not long after. Since then she has married again.

I also went with a lady for two years named Barbara who was really devoted to me and would have been the most wonderful partner. But unfortunately, I didn't love her, and it was her I had left for Marlene.

Jane and I met at a PWP dance not long after Marlene. We went together for a few months but I was not over Marlene. She sensed it, and although we never had anything serious going, we have remained friends and still email and visit as I write this. I went to her wedding on October 23rd in 1998. She married Dave and he seems to be a nice person and I hope they stay happy together.

Chapter 12

RETIREMENT

Bob and youngest Mike, fixing their co-owned rental property

I retired from Boeing ten days after my sixty-fifth birthday. I had worked there twenty-one years and the last fifteen with perfect attendance. I had been counting down the days like many people do. I had plans to be a Host on the cruise lines; build a house on my ten acres on Getchel Hill in Lake Stevens; and many other things. I had been trying to get permission to build on my property for a number of years.

The latest hold up was the property had been selected as a potential site for a much-needed airport in the north to support SeaTac. I had also been trying to subdivide the ten acres into two fives. Due to the wetland on some of the property, I was involved in a lot of complications in surveying and mapping the wet areas and obtaining permits for the well drilling, installing the drain-field, and building the road. It was a continuous fight with the county planning office. There were fees for the Surveyor, Biologist, Civil Engineer, Lawyers, drain-field design, general permits and other fees. The sub division fee amounted in total to $36,000. This was an expenditure that was necessary before the house was even started.

It took six years from starting with the first surveyor to the approval of the subdivision. This was mostly for paperwork. The house was finally finished in May of 1995. That was one of my retirement goals achieved.

My second retirement goal was to be a Cruise Line Host. I started by going to a travel agent I know and asked them for as much information about cruise lines as possible. They searched their travel books that listed all the cruise lines and they photo copied me a list of all the potential cruise lines that use hosts. I composed a letter to send to them all, giving them references and my experiences that could be beneficial to becoming a Host. It worked as I was offered an interview with The Royal Viking Cruise line. I was to go to Coral Gables to their main office at my own expense for my first interview.

It was quite an expensive fare, over four hundred dollars, but I decided it would be worth it. I arrived one evening for the 10:00 A.M. interview the next day. I was interviewed by a man and woman and asked a lot of questions and it seemed to go well. The next step was to go to their local Arthur Murray studio for a dancing evaluation, which also went well. There were five other applicants, some of them could hardly dance from what I could see. We had to dance around the floor to a quick step, rumba and waltz. The other applicants just went around the floor once with the instructor, but she kept me for a number of turns around, so I felt happy about it.

I bet the other guys hated me.

After a couple of weeks, I received a letter saying I would be called to go on a cruise for them. Time went by and I heard nothing. Finally, I decided to contact the Royal Cruise Line in San Francisco and see if they could use me seeing as I had been accepted for Royal Viking and they were a subsidiary of Royal Viking. It worked and they invited me to take my first cruise.

It was the first of many enjoyable cruises. It started in Acapulco and finished in Aruba going through the Panama Canal. It was the only seven-day cruise I went on. The ship was the Golden Odyssey, Royal Viking's smallest ship. I got on well with the cruise director and everything went very well. I will not go into any detail about the cruise. I will spend more time describing "hosting" in the next chapter.

The house I wanted to build was on my mind. I knew exactly what I wanted so I went to a local builder, O'Connor & Oehler. They were an older, well-established builder in the area. I looked at some of the plans he had to offer that he had built in the area. I went to one of the houses they had built to see what sort of job they did. I took home one of the plans they had built that was about the size of house I wanted.

I spent the next couple of weeks drawing a set of plans. I designed the layout to my satisfaction completely drawing it on Mylar from beginning to end. I took it to O'Connor and had it estimated. The quote was $68,000. I sent it to another builder and he was much higher so I was happy for O'Connor and Oehler to get it started.

We started by sending the plans into the county planning and building office and going through all the necessary permits again. The permit was finally released to start without a change to my plan. I came out to the site one morning with Nita, my Norwegian dancing friend, and we found the surveyors markers and were able to put in stakes where the corner of the garage and house were to be. Before we started, the County Planners came out with the builders and all agreed on the location of the stakes and we finally started moving earth.

It was about November when we got the final start date, just as the rain started and then the frost. It was after Christmas before the foundation was poured and floor in place. I was on a month or so cruise and didn't get back until it was done. Due to the weather, they still dragged their feet, and I was concerned that the rain and snow would have some ill effects on the wood floor. It didn't. Time has proven that. I asked the builder for a possible completion date and he said he would be hoping for May.

That gave me an idea for a date to sell the house on Panaview Boulevard in Valley View, Everett, WA. The date also helped me to know when I would be around to purchase the carpet and supervise the finishing touches. I had said I didn't want any vinyl veneer instead of wood and a number of other things that I needed to be there and watch for. I had planned to do the tile around the fireplace myself. I put Panaview on the market in March attempting to sell it without an agent but nothing happened. The house next door had been up for sale for ages and hadn't moved so I picked one of the agents that been pestering me and decided on a price.

I then left on a 35-day cruise. I received an offer by Fax while I was at sea in the Mediterranean. I sent a counter offer that was accepted and it was sold. I had a hassle with the Greek radio operator on the ship but in spite of him, I got all the communications satisfactorily resolved and was able to sleep that night knowing it was all taken care of.

Panaview was due for possession on May 20th so with the help of the family, we were moved into the new house by the 16th and everything was completed by then. I have been very pleased with the room layout, construction, and insulation. I had a wood stove installed and the place has been easy to heat and comfortable. I had a 30 x 30-foot workshop built that worked out really well for all my needs and it fits in well with the house.

Chapter 13

CRUISE LINE HOST

Hosting on Cruise Lines during retirement. Many travels all over the world.

My first cruise was from Acapulco to Aruba on the Golden Odyssey, a small cruise ship that carried 450 passengers. I received instructions and all the information necessary to carry out my duties as a host. I arrived at the port of embarkation on time. I was in a cabin with another Host who had done many trips. He was not very sociable or helpful. We had to be at certain functions at given times and he would see me walking in the wrong direction and not tell me. However, I did well without his help and got on well with the cruise director and was accepted as a permanent host for the line.

The Cruise Line considers a Host to be an independent contractor and not an employee of the Cruise Line. The Cruise Line will provide a round trip economy fare to the port of embarkation and return fare from port of disembarkation. The specific airline, date and time of departure are the sole discretion of the Cruise Line. There are no deviations to the ticket provided.

A stateroom is provided for the Host to be shared with another Host, at the discretion of the Line. Hosts are to be assigned to back-to-back cruises for a period of 30-40 days at a time. Hosts are provided with all services, meals, entertainment and receptions, which are provided in the paying passenger's contract. Hosts may be required to escort shore excursions at the discretion of the Shore Excursion Manager. Requests to accompany shore excursions may be requested and are also at the discretion of the Shore Excursion Manager dependant on space available. Hosts may purchase excursions if they wish.

Hosts are expected to serve as ex-officio part of the cruise staff without compensation. The Host's responsibility is to host all single ladies, ages 50 and over, with particular emphasis on the following: General companion, General partner, A Dancing partner, A partner in games including bridge other card games. Also, backgammon and deck games and be a participant in shore excursions as assigned and any other duties requested by the Cruise Director. All ladies are to be treated equally with no favouritism.

All Hosts will conduct themselves in a gentlemanly manner at all times for the duration of the cruise. A Host must provide himself with an adequate wardrobe consisting of a black Tux, white dinner jacket, and appropriate sports clothes. Hosts should look their best at all times. Hosts will be assigned to a table in the dining room by the Maître d' and will serve as Host at a table of single ladies at breakfast, lunch, and dinner as assigned. They will be responsible to rotate between tables. Hosts will remain in the dance areas as assigned to dance with all single ladies 50 and older, as directed by the cruise director, or staff. Crystal Cruise Line has a 14-page manual for their Hosts and this is the section on fraternising with passengers beyond the Host duties.

Quote: "It is a fact that there is a disproportionate number of women compared to men on luxury cruises, and hence a major factor why this program exists."

It also states that cruising and romance go together, like bread and butter, like soup and salad. Think oil and water. You may be tempted to dally in matters that exceed the extent of this program. Not unlike small towns, there are no secrets, people will talk, people will know. If you dally not only will you be in the doghouse, you will be asked to dog paddle to the next port and find your own way home from there. It is this simple: do not dally!

"Crystal Cruise Line does not tolerate any personal romantic relationships while you are on board in the capacity of Ambassador Host. What you do after you get back home is your business. If you want to exchange addresses and keep in contact with people you meet on board after you get back home, that of course, is up to you. But always remember that you are on the host program, and you must not, under any circumstances, pursue any personal relationships while you are serving on board as an Ambassador Host and a representative of the Crystal Cruise Line. You should not show special attention to one woman at the expense of slighting another, even if they request it."

The Hosts became quite well known before a cruise was over. We started with introductions from the stage at the beginning of the cruise. On the second day out, we had a singles party and were again introduced. Then during the cruise there was a picture and write up in the ship's newspaper giving details of our background, where we came from, our profession, education and hobbies etc. We also had to mix with people throughout the trip including all mealtimes. I heard many life stories and details of people's lives. On a cruise people in general are more secure and are much more friendly and open to making friends and talking freely. As a Host on approximately thirty Cruises, during which I visited sixty different countries, I had the pleasure of dancing and becoming acquainted with about eighteen hundred ladies at a conservative average of sixty per cruise. We also had to mix with people at other times besides at meal time. Below is my "Introduction".

Gentleman Host- Robert E. Scanes
Seattle, Washington

Bob was born in England and his British manner tempered with an outgoing American-style friendliness makes him pleasant and interesting company. He is fit and well proportioned, and his ballroom dancing experience started at the age of sixteen where he studied with the "British Imperial School of Dancing".

He was raised in England and experienced the blitz in the London area. He served as Aircrew in the RAF for six years. Due to the Suez Canal crises, which resulted in rationing being reintroduced, Bob emigrated with his wife and daughter to Montreal, Canada, in 1957, where he was Employed by Canadair and then Rolls Royce of Canada as an Assistant Quality Engineer.

He continued his education at McGill University in Montreal and was recruited in 1968 by Boeing as an Industrial Engineer, where he worked until he retired in 1990. After divorce in 1975, Bob learned to make the best of single life. He has many interests including teaching X/C skiing for two months every year, photography, wine making, cooking, buying and renovating rental property. He is in the process of moving into a house he has just built on ten acres in Lake Stevens, thirty miles north of Seattle. He could have completely built the house himself but says, "Life is too short".

Here is an example of typical activity on a flight to a port of embarkation.

This cruise was to start from Malaga, Spain, and we were leaving Seattle in the winter. I left SeaTac in reasonably good weather heading to my first destination, New York. We had picked a bad time to go. New York had a heavy snow storm and when we arrived it was still difficult to land. There was a blizzard, and just as we landed, a cross wind hit the plane and we were really lucky we made it safely. The airport had been closed for three days and there were still masses of people laying around and sleeping on seats.

We arrived at Kennedy Airport and had to transfer to the international concourse which was about three miles away. There were about thirty people directed to the place. We picked up the transport. A cruise line representative was there to direct us. He led the group, who were mainly older people, some in wheelchairs and using walkers. Finally, we arrived at the exit. There were still large piles of snow and quite a lot of slush on the ground. Our shuttle bus arrived at the Iberia concourse and we trudged through the slush into the terminal to exchange our tickets. After waiting an hour, we were finally on the plane and again we were waiting to take off. There were a lot of planes in line, and it was about a half hour before we were off. I heard later that others were there for three or four hours.

I was lucky I was sitting next to a very pleasant lady; she was about forty-six and lived in New Jersey. She was travelling with her youngest daughter to Madrid to visit the eldest daughter who was studying engineering at Madrid University. Three months earlier she had split from her husband of twenty-five years. We talked for nearly the whole flight in spite of being tired. She was working as a teacher and had her masters and was studying for her doctorate. When we parted at Madrid airport, I felt I had really helped her with her feelings towards her husband and her adjustment to her new single life. I think we both felt really close to each other in a way in spite of our age difference and that our paths would never cross again.

I have met many people on flights whose company I enjoyed. Due to a good tail wind, we arrived in Madrid with four hours to kill for our next flight. Madrid airport was no exception to all the others. It required a mile walk from one concourse to the other. The four hours was necessary for some of the passengers to get to the right concourse. They changed the gate number three times before we boarded the plane. This being a domestic flight, we were flying in a 727 that they had filled to capacity. I had a window seat with two men sitting beside me who slept most of the way. I twice tried to take a video and was told by the steward it was not permitted. I remember the ground was rolling hills that were varying shades of red and other colours and I wanted to record them. I did eventually get video of it. It was an uneventful flight and everyone was happy when we touched down at Malaga. It was a big relief to see my luggage and to know I had my clothes. It wasn't uncommon for a Host to have to go a few days because his luggage was lost and they had to try to borrow clothes from other hosts. There at last was the ship. What a welcome sight.

The Royal Odyssey was built in 1962 and purchased by the Royal Cruise Line in 1991 when it was refitted for extended service. It was 28,000 tons with 410 staterooms and held 765 passengers, and 410 crew. A nice ship but she had seen better days.

The cabin I was assigned to was number 3069, deck 3, amidships and an outside cabin with two portholes. I was to share it with another Host, John Witherspoon, who was working for two other Cruise Lines, Crystal and Royal Viking. John was signed up for four cruises on this ship. He seemed to be pushing a little hard and said he needed to slow down and get a rest.

We had seven hosts on that cruise which was the right amount for the ladies in the dance area. A host's dancing ability ranged about as much as the ladies from poor to not too bad. The cruise can't afford to be picky as there are not enough good dancers available with the other Host requirements.

The average age of the hosts was about 65. We had one, 82 years old, who danced quite well and was a real pleasant person. He had a serious hearing problem and nodded and smiled a lot. When he was on the dance floor, he was a danger and stepped on a lot of toes. The senior Host on this cruise didn't dance to the same drummer as me. I watched the poor women trying to dance with him and blaming themselves. I felt sorry for them. He had been cruising for a long time and getting away with it. Lording himself over the other Hosts and looking at them through his thick glasses with his stuffy serious attitude and lack of dancing ability.

One morning at open seating breakfast, I was seated next to two young ladies from Ottawa who I talked with. They were wondering who they would like to take advantage of the Hosts to dance with. At lunch when we were on tour, we ate at the Hyatt Regency. After lunch at the buffet, I sat at one of the many tables next to one of the other Hosts and who should it be that table sitting down next to us but the two breakfast table ladies.

We talked again and I suggested they might like to join the Hosts in the dancing area in the evening. So that evening the smaller of the two was there. She wasn't a dancer but it was surprising how quickly she learnt. She really took a fancy to me and was really persistent to spend time with me dancing and didn't want to share me with the other ladies. She was really affectionate and it was difficult not to hurt her feelings. It was heading to more of a problem as the cruise continued. I told her that being a Host I was already giving her more attention than I should and managed to slow her down without upsetting her. Keeping certain ladies happy without them reading more into it than was intended, was difficult at times. Fortunately, they nearly always lived on the other side of the country. It all worked out okay with the French nurse from Ottawa. I wrote to her for a while but it dropped off.

I made it a goal to enjoy every dance, regardless of the lady's ability to dance. I have had a lot of dancing lessons and dancing experience during my life, and I lead my partners very positively but lightly. When I dance with a new lady, I first determine if she knows the rhythm she is dancing to. I then decide if I should just follow her or count. Slow, slow-quick, quick-slow or one, two, three, depending on the dance. If a lady does respond to my lead, I follow for a while and talk to her. Then if I think it appropriate, I ask her if she would like me to help her to get started. For many of the ladies it is the first time they have danced in years and then they are pleased to be helped. But I was always very cautious. Once they feel their feet there's no looking back.

I remember once on an Alaska Cruise on the Golden Odyssey, there were not that many ladies, but two I remember in particular. It's funny how some stand out in my memory. They were at the dance area from the minute the band started until the very end of the evening. They kept us up to dance with them alone until the last when we all should have called it a night. Sometimes two of us would call it a night leaving two to dance with them. When the dance area finally emptied and it was late, the band would stop playing and we would have an early night. When there was a crowd, we were happy to stay up and enjoy it with them. On one cruise, there were two hangers-on.

These particular two ladies could dance. One was okay at swing, so I said to the other, "If you would like me to help you, you could swing as well as your friend". So, I counted for her, and in no time had her twisting around and getting back in step for a change. I was quite pleased with her improvement and thought she was also. I had been very discrete when I helped her and not made it obvious.

Later that evening I got her for another swing dance and she started with her previous problems so I thought I would count for her again. You wouldn't believe how bent out of shape she got. I said, "I am sorry. I won't offer to help again." For the rest of the cruise when I had to dance with her, I avoided swing dances and you can be sure I just followed and was polite. Goodness knows what got into her. I think that was the only time I had that problem. I had learnt my lesson about giving too much advice.

During the time I was a Host I knew of only a few times that one of the Hosts took the chance to have an obvious romance during a cruise. The opportunity was there most cruises. It was not uncommon to have a lady suggest that you accompany her to her cabin or offer to go to yours. It wasn't often direct and usually after you got to know them towards the end of the cruise. Most of them knew the rules that applied to the Hosts. They may have been just trying to see if we kept to them.

One Japanese lady came alone on a cruise and I made an effort to make her trip enjoyable. Yoshiko couldn't speak very much English, but I listened to her carefully and we communicated reasonably well. Yoshiko would come in the dance area and wait until I danced with her. If any of the other Hosts asked her, she refused. After a dance she would go and come back later and wait until I asked to dance with her again. When there was a tour, she asked me what bus I was going on. Usually, I didn't know. She would wait around until I got to a bus, then come and sit with me. It became quite a joke with the other Hosts. I told her the rules we had and it worked out and I didn't mind her company, I wasn't trying to make time with anyone else.

Yoshiko was on the twenty-eight-day cruise from Athens to Singapore. I must have told her I was going on it and she booked the cruise later to be with me. She said she owned a 250-bed hospital in Tokyo. That was a good cruise but I had two ladies on it that were there because it was a good itinerary and so they could dance with me. I had to be especially careful that neither could complain

We went to Athens (Port of Piraeus) where we had seen the acropolis. It was one of my chosen ports to shop for shoes. I bought some patent leather, dress shoes and a beautiful pair of white shoes with leather soles for dancing to use with my blue blazer and white pants. Our next port of call was Ashdod, the port we always docked to visit Bethlehem, Jerusalem, and Tel Aviv, which was always a pleasure. There was always the fear of terrorists. One time before we sailed, skin divers searched the bottom of the ship to make sure there were no bombs on it.

When we went into Jerusalem there was a big gate and we were searched before we could enter. The first thing to see was the Wailing Wall. The wall was divided with a small barrier partly for men and the other for the women. We would go there to walk the Seven Stations of the Cross. On a previous visit we had stopped to go on the usual walk and it was raining hard. I said to one of the other Hosts, "What shall we do?" he said. "If once was enough for Jesus, once is enough for me".

Once I was there and it was a Greek religious day and everyone was dressed in black robes and flat black hats. A bell was tolling and a group was carrying a large wooden cross. I have a video of it and it is quite impressive. I went to the place of Christ's birth in the church in Bethlehem. We got into the Manger and they shuffled everyone out except five of us. They started a service singing and waving incense.

I was a few feet from the spot where Christ was born. I didn't take a video as it said videos were okay, but not of services and monks. My conscience got the better of me. My visit to Tel Aviv was not a tour organized by the ship but with four of the lady passengers we took a taxi there and went to an art display and wandered the stores. The only thing I bought was a cup, which has since been broken. Our next port of call was Port Said Egypt; at last, I was to see the pyramids from the ground. It was an interesting tour. On the way we went into a large mosque which was very interesting and I upset a few passengers by being late back to the coach. I was haggling with one on the locals for something and when I got back on the coach, they all started clapping. For something like that we could lose our job as a Host. Passengers can be weird sometimes if they take a disliking to you.

We went to a hotel for lunch as soon as we arrived in Cairo and watched dancing girls during the meal. From there we went to the pyramids and the sphinx. It was really interesting to see the actual size being there. I thought the Pyramids were unbelievably large and the sphinx small. From there we went to the Cairo Museum and saw many interesting items including Mummies with gold masks. I bought a number of parchment drawings.

The next morning, we arose sailing through the Suez Canal. By midday we had arrived at one of the Bitter Lakes where we dropped anchor to wait for ships sailing in the opposite direction to clear the way for us. This turned out to be a problem as we were scheduled to arrive at Eilat, Israel, our next port early enough to go on tour to Mount Sinai. I should have liked to go on that tour but as it was, no one went. We were shown around the town and taken to an aquarium. It had a stairway to go down below the sea that had glass we could look through and see the native fish.

Our next port of call was Port Safaga. There were coaches waiting for us and we were immediately on our way. It was a long winding road through the mountains that looked like gravel – not a blade of grass. This was another area where terrorists were feared. We were going fast all the time and there were armed jeeps with seven guns sticking out, in front and behind guarding our convoy of coaches in case a band of terrorists attacked us.

We stopped at roadblocks and the armed guards checked us over. We eventually came to more interesting country and finally arrived at Luxor. We crossed the Nile on a ferry and proceeded to the Valley of the Kings. Archaeologists had found different tombs hidden in the hills. The one we entered had a cement entrance and we were allowed to go down and see what remained of the treasures. We saw a mummy laying in a stone coffin, the same as we had seen in the Cairo Museum without going down a hole to see it. I wouldn't recommend anyone to bother making the journey on the gravel roads with armed guards.

From the valley we went to a big stone temple that was worth the visit with a line of stone tigers leading up to it. The tour guide was not very good and said we couldn't make a video. When we got there after a long walk, all the other groups had their video cameras. I had my 35mm.

From there we had three days at sea to get to Bombay. We had a day to look around Bombay. We wandered around the city for a few hours and visited the Taj Hotel. It was a very amazing place. We had to pay to go on this tour which was something I hadn't done before – $750.

We flew to New Delhi and spent the night at a very nice hotel. Yoshiko was on the tour so seeing I was paying for the tour, I considered I was on my own time so I spent a fair amount of time with her.

From New Delhi we went by train to Agra. We were there early and went by coach directly to the Taj Mahal. It was the most beautiful building I had ever seen, so clean and undamaged. It was all white marble and decorated with a pattern of semi-precious stones. It was started in 1612 and completed in 1648, built by Prince Khurram the fifth Mughal emperor, a monument of eternal love, to perpetuate the memory of his wife Mumtaz Mahal.

After our visit to the Taj, we went to a nice hotel where we had a delicious lunch, which was followed by another coach tour to a big Palace that was built prior to the Taj, but never occupied because there was a long drought. It was interesting but nothing to talk much about. The journey was interesting, going through Indian villages to see the locals in their daily life. I got some good video.

We returned to New Delhi by train. We toured around New Delhi where there were many beautiful buildings built by the English and now maintained by India. Our guide had a lot of good things to say about the English giving the impression the English occupation was not negative. We flew from to New Delhi direct to Goa, and though we had been advised to be careful what we ate, I had no bad effect from the food. We arrived at Goa the same morning as the boat, so we were able to go on the passenger tour to a very beautiful church and there was a special festival going on there that was celebrated only once every ten years.

A Saint Francis embalmed body was taken from a tomb and on display. We were able to file past it. It was amazingly well preserved. It was on this cruise we had a guy get into an obvious romance. This was the longest cruise I did with the same ladies, twenty-eight days. People were beginning to get too close and know too much about each other. One of the Hosts had a real strong romance going. To the extent it was obvious to everyone when we went on shore. At one port, the lady bought him an expensive present. The Assistant Cruise Director and Senior Host discussed the situation and the Host was warned. The woman was a pleasant person and terrible flirt. To divert attention from her relationship with the other Host, she started coming on to me. I had become friendly enough with her and her sister. Her sister was totally different, older and knew her sister well. I was able to tell her with her sister there, that I could see through her attention to me and make a joke of it. We became good friends and I have written to her since. She lives in Park Lane, NY.

Our next two ports after Goa were Colombo, then Madras. We went ashore and were shown around, but I don't remember anything outstanding. Port Blair was the next stop and it was on an island and was much more interesting. I don't think they had many ships stop there because there was a crowd to meet us. We went first to a school where all the children were having lessons. I had brought a big red delicious apple off the ship with me and gave it to one of the teachers. All the children spoke French and were in uniform. It seemed like a good school and they were as interested in us as we in them.

In one of the classrooms, they had a choir singing that was really good. From there we went to a big old jail that had been there for years. All the cells looked out from a balcony that was built in a half circle. During World War II, the Japanese used it for a prisoner of war camp.

There was a fancy gallows built of stone with two hanging ropes side by side with trap doors so they could hang two at a time. It was really interesting and strange to think so many had died by those gallows. I wish I had more information on it.

The next port was Phuket, Thailand, which was not close enough for us to go on tour to Bangkok. Instead, we were in a beautiful tourist area with large hotels. We did have a chance to go over a cashew nut processing area. The shells were strong and each contained one nut that had to be opened using a small press then each nut was hand scraped then cooked in a large pan prior to packing – no wonder they are so expensive.

We were taken to one of the large hotels for a meal, then wandered around the grounds and swimming pools and down to the beach where I noticed the ladies were swimming with no tops. We had only one stop between there and Singapore, Penang, and I think that is where we saw a large reclining Buddha. Next we went to a company that was making special tie-dyed fabrics to make dresses and sarongs.

Our next port was Singapore, where Yoshiko left the ship and stayed over in a hotel for a couple of days prior to flying home. I was able to stay with her for a while. While we were there, we went on the cable car to the island and saw an aquarium, the best I have ever seen. It was a glass tube with the water all around and there was a moving conveyor to stand on that just slowly carries you through the aquarium. You can step off the catwalk with the video camera running and get a nice clear picture of it all. Sharks, mantras and hundreds of fish I didn't recognise. There was a butterfly building with masses of butterflies that settled on people.

While I was in Singapore, I went on a tour to Raffles Hotel, a very well-known hotel, especially for their drink called a Singapore Sling.

Singapore Sling recipe from Raffles Hotel

1 ½ ounces gin
½ ounce cherry heering liquer
¼ ounce Cointreau liqueur
¼ ounce Benedictine
4 ounces pineapple juice
½ ounce lime juice
1/3-ounce grenadine
1 dash bitters
Shake with ice. Strain into ice filled Collins glasses. Garnish With cherry and a slice of pineapple.

Yoshiko and I met about a half a mile from the hotel and travelled the rest of the way in a trishaw. It was good to be peddled to the hotel. We went to the bar and were all served a Singapore Sling. I bought a glass with the name written on it. Singapore is such a clean city and has very strict laws and harsh punishments. It was even safe for ladies to walk the streets at night because if anyone was caught harming them, they would go to jail for life, and may even get lashed with the cat of nine tails as well. The following year Yoshiko took a vacation in Vancouver and I met her there. I stayed with her and we went golfing and ate at a nice rotating restaurant. We wrote for a while but after the accident we stopped.

I met a lot of really pleasant ladies and would go on tours with them always making sure I wasn't seen with them very often. Wanda, from Ontario and I met on a cruise and we became good friends and spent a lot of time together. We visited each other's homes and met our families. I met a great number of very special people on the cruises, not just ladies, but couples at my table and other ways. People I will be friends with and correspond with for life.

I met a lady from Melbourne travelling with her sister and brother-in-law on a cruise from Hong Kong to Singapore and became very close to the family. I had a cold on that cruise and they insisted I needed a double to help cure it. The lady's name is Nelly and I write to her regularly.

We docked in Melbourne on a later cruise and I was able to go on a tour that went along the street where she lived. I wasn't able to visit, so I sent her a card.

Our next port of call was Hobart, Tasmania. When we arrived, I had a fax saying how sorry she was she missed me. On a later cruise I met another lady who lived very close to her on the same street and I introduced them by mail and they got together and became friends.

During my cruises I went to many places. I will just write about the ones I recall as special and most enjoyable.

Each time I have been through the Panama Canal I have enjoyed it. It takes about eight hours and the ship is always full of first timers and they make it more interesting. There is a commentary and films on how it was built and works. The canal was first surveyed by Spanish King Charles 1st in 1543. The first attempt to build it was by the French in 1880, but due to their method and the problem with sickness it was discounted. The United States started in 1903 and after a lot of loss of life and problems it was completed.

I have a list of all the ports I visited and the number of times. I have a video of nearly every port I visited. When I look back on my cruises and all the places I visited, certain special ports and tours come to mind. The Panama Canal Cruise was my first, which I eventually did four times. Prior to entering the canal from the west, Panama City can be seen on the starboard side. It looks like a big beautiful city, but as I write this, American citizens are not welcome.

The Panama Cruise is a very popular one and worth mentioning as it is a frequent first cruise for passengers. The canal itself was a big part of the cruise, but some of the other ports had things to offer. When the ship came up to the locks it was taken in tow by four cables from electric trains called ponies. One was connected each side at the bow and one on each side at the stern to hold the ship in a fixed position within the lock and take complete control while the ship is going through. This control keeps the ship from touching the sides because some ships only have inches to spare and the ponies control the ship within inches of the lock gates and sides.

The cables keep taught and keep the ship in place as the water rises or falls. There is a movie that shows the history on the different approaches, designs and on how many attempts were made to build it. It shows the people and engineering problems they had with sicknesses like malaria.

Due to the climate and mosquitoes, 25.000 people died building it. The amount of earth and rock moved was colossal. All the time the ship is travelling through the canal there is a commentary on the various things of interest that can be seen from the deck. There is a river running into the canal at the east end so the canal is fresh water. As the excess water is released to control the level of the canal it is used for a Hydroelectric plant that supplies all the power necessary to run the Ponies and locks.

Prior to entering the Panama Canal from the West, we visited Acapulco. The cliff divers were worth seeing. It is obviously a big commercial operation. The divers have a union and only they are allowed to dive. They start on lower levels of the cliff and gradually work their way up until they graduate to the top level. There is a little shrine at the top and to stretch the show they say a little prayer and stand on the edge for a while before they dive. It was said no one has ever been killed diving there. They do three or four shows a day and only the people who have paid can get to the vantage point to actually see the diver. There is only one dive at each show. After the dive the diver comes in among the audience. It is a tour from the Cruise Line that costs way more than the admission to the observation point, but the passengers are taken there in a coach and returned to the ship.

We next docked at Puerto Quetzal, Guatemala, and went into town there. They were hand-making beautiful tapestries. I bought an attractive piece, but I think that it was machine made because I didn't pay the price of a handmade item. The place was very dirty and it looked as if they dumped their garbage along the side of the roads on the way in and out of the city. There was a lot of poverty and it was not a safe place to be alone.

Another port was Caldera, Costa Rica. We visited San Jose and went into a big palace with beautiful gardens. We saw a show of beautiful young girls folk dancing in lovely dresses. On the way home from that tour I had an embarrassing experience. While we were on the coach, we were given numbers to place on the table so when we went into lunch we had a seat, then we would line up for the meal and go back to the place we had chosen. That was okay, but when I returned to my table where I had placed my number, one of the passengers came to the table and insisted that I had his seat. I was at a loss as there were no

140

extra seats and he was insistent. I had to wait until everyone was back to see what seats were left.

It finally worked out, and later his wife came to me and apologized. We also went to a coffee plantation where I bought some coffee beans.

Other ports of call on that trip that were of interest on the east end of the canal were the San Blas Islands. They are two islands between the east end of the canal and Curacao. They are interesting because they are still very primitive. Natives still live in grass huts and survive on the Cruise Lines visiting to sell their goods. Their main items made by hand are what they call Mola, which are beautiful patterns on cloth. The hand stitching on some of them were very intricate, and they priced them accordingly. I was interested in one but I couldn't negotiate a good price, so I didn't buy anything.

Aruba is a popular tourist trap, and I cannot see what people see in the place. It is flat with nothing other than the sun, gambling, hotels, and scuba diving to see the many fish. I visited many Islands in the Caribbean and did not find enough interest to want to go back for. When I visited Bonaire, I did go on a submarine tour that was interesting. About thirty of us were taken out to the submarine. We climbed down the ladder into the long narrow interior with windows on each side and a large window at the front.

It was electrically powered and the motor could be heard operating the ventilation fans. When we were all settled, they shut down the hatch and we headed down. There was a hill under the water and we were able to circle around it about twenty feet below the surface and look out at the coral and fish and other underwater terrain that was at that level. There were brilliant coloured fish and coral.

We started at 25 feet deep, then we submerged to one hundred and fifty feet. It got darker and there was not much new to see. Not as much was living at that level. The end of the runway of the local airfield finished just where the submarine started. I saw they were dumping rubbish into the water right at the end of the runway. If this continues, I thought, "They won't have the fish here for long."

Chapter 14

ACCIDENT

Rufous and great companion after my accident.

On August 26, 1996, I was working on a new building that had been constructed on my ten acres. I was installing an attic floor and was down to the last sheet of 8x4 wafer board when somehow, I will never know how, I slipped and fell ten feet on my back and fractured my spine in three places. There was a lot of wood scraps laying on the floor and I think I must have landed on one of them. It is a 30'x30' metal building with 10'x10' and a 9'x7' garage door.

Fortunately, the ten-foot door was open. As soon as I came around,

I tried to sum up my situation but must have still been confused. I had a cut on my head that eventually needed ten stitches. My left hand had two serious cuts on the fingers and I was paralyzed from just above my waist down.

I have no idea how long I laid there unconscious.

The first time I remember looking at my watch it was about 11:00 A.M. It must have been about 10.00 A.M. when it happened. I live out in the country and sometimes I don't see anyone for days. I realized I may lie there for days and could die of hypothermia if I didn't take some action to prevent that from happening.

Although I was fully aware that with a spinal cord injury, I could cause additional injury if I moved, I decide that was what I had to do. There was a roll of six-foot-wide plastic-backed insulation in the middle of the floor about 14 feet from where I lay. Even though I knew it was not right to move I decided my best bet was to try to it. Somehow, I managed to roll, slide and drag myself across the floor until I reached it. I can remember how restricted I was at the time, and I am sure I did not cause any further injury.

The neighbor's dog, a large black lab, was there and was licking my wounds. I was concerned she would make a meal of my fingers. They were like minced meat so I decided to keep them away from her. I tried to get help from her and our dog. But it was of no avail. Neither would even lay with me and keep me warm. They just wanted to bring me sticks to throw. I got to the insulation, leaving a trail of blood. I tore up some clear plastic hardware bags and bound my fingers. There were some pieces of wood and plasterboard on the floor so I managed to get onto that to get myself off the cold cement floor, then I wrapped myself in the plastic insulation ready for the long night wait.

It was surprising how quickly the time passed. At 5:00 P.M. I heard my neighbors on their horses, out on their evening ride. They have a trail on their property through the woods about twenty to thirty feet from the property line. They would have been about 75 plus yards from where I lay. It was a silent evening and I could hear nearly every word they were saying. This is my chance I thought. I shouted at the top of my voice, "Help help". But unfortunately, they rode on and I heard their voices fade in the distance.

I settled down for another wait with the thought again of being there for the night. Then at 7:00 I could hear them again. This was my last hope. There were some thick brown paper hardware bags near me, so I emptied the hardware from one of them, flattened it out then rolled it in a cone to make a megaphone so my voice would carry to them better. After 3 or 4 calls they heard me and came over to see what the problem was.

I was saved! Saved for a fate worse than dying.

The police ambulance, fire department and everyone was there. In no time I was laid on a backboard and trussed up so I couldn't move a muscle and put in the ambulance and away. They took me to Cascade Hospital in Arlington about fifteen miles from my home; dressed my cuts: and put me in a plastic neck brace and did whatever else they could. It was then I decided I should be sent to the main trauma hospital in the area, Harborview in Seattle.

They flew me there by helicopter, about forty miles. By the time we were ready to take off, my whole family had arrived at the hospital soon to drive to Harborview to meet me there. The two attendants in the helicopter were very friendly and pleasant. It was dark by the time we arrived. We landed on the roof of the next building over from the main hospital. I had numerous x-rays and MRI's and it was determined I had injured C-6&7 and T4. My condition was, "T4 incomplete", meaning that I had loss of mobility from my chest down.

The doctors could see no damage to my spinal cord and said they were surprised I had so much trauma for the amount of injury that showed on the MRI. To keep me stable with the injury, I was to be trapped in a Halo for twelve weeks. With the paralysis not being total, there was some feeling and movement. I was then drilled into the Halo, a plastic bodice that was tight around my chest and down to the waist with four metal rods that came up one on each side of the face and two behind the head. This allowed a ring to be fitted around the head from each the rods. From the ring, four screws were fitted that screwed into my skull to keep the head stable and stop the head and spine from moving. It was painful enough having the screws tightened into the skull, but the doctor did not remove the hair as he turned the screws – it pulled out the hair.

I got upset and told him he was a sadist, which he didn't forget when he visited during the rest of my stay at Harborview. Perhaps he remembered enough to take pity on the next one he installed.

I was in Harborview for about eight days and the time went quickly.

The nurses were wonderful to me. Certainly nothing to complain about there. My stay at Harborview with all the other trauma patients lasted for seven days. I must say, the care and attention were the best. Everyone was very pleasant and capable. It was then that they decided I was ready for physical therapy and should be moved. Another ambulance ride on a backboard in an ambulance with four square wheels, 70 pounds in each tire.

I had been given the choice of three hospitals for rehabilitation, so I decided to go to Providence Hospital in Everett, the nearest to my home and the family and friends who would visit me. I didn't know I had so many friends.

I received over fifty cards, heaps of flowers and potted plants. Lots of people were at my bedside. I just wished I could have transformed all the good feelings and well wishes into some kind of get-well potion to help all the pain and discomfort go away. Unfortunately, it does not work that way. Physical Therapy is to rebuild the muscles, balance, methods of exercise and teach a person to make the best of their physical situation. It is a lot of hard work pushing you to the limits – sometimes beyond.

Occupational Therapy was to adapt me to function at home alone, teach me to dress myself and use the conveniences as well as to transfer to a wheelchair from the bed and in and out of a car, using a slide board. The instructors were mostly young, very conscientious and pleasant. At times I felt like a prisoner sentenced to hard labour when I was forced to get up and work when I was hurting and wanted to rest.

The Halo made me sore and uncomfortable the more I moved around in it. I was on medication that made me thirsty and nauseous, causing me to lose my appetite.

The idea of rehabilitation is to make a person as independent as possible and that is what they do. As the time goes on, the nurses give you less and less help and attention.   Unfortunately, sometimes it is less than is necessary, making life quite hard at times. Fortunately, the few special nurses that became friends and went beyond the call of duty made my life bearable. The time finally came for me to go home. Before this could happen, my house had to be adapted for wheelchair use by widening doors, building a ramp so I could get in and out, and many other things like getting a hospital bed. Home help had to be arranged. Everything was inspected and proven, which took at least two visits with the Occupational Therapist.

My family orchestrated and helped with the adaptation of the house. Finally, the day came. I had been in Providence for forty days. It was October 11th. My daughter, Carole, and former wife, Mavis (still a good friend), were there to help me into Mavis' Honda Accord and take me home.

My first month at home has been long and tedious, enduring the Halo and all the other restrictions. Without my good and wonderful friend Lilian, whom I have known for about five years, I am sure it would have been unbearable. She has been my right hand and three quarters of my left hand, cooking, cleaning and helping me in every way possible.

November 14 was the day we were to go to Harborview and have the Halo removed. We were up at 6:00 A.M. We decided to go in my Acura, using the slide board to get into it. Getting in and out of the really low car was not easy. At 8:00, we were on the road with my daughter Carole driving. I cannot say enough about the help and the moral support I have had from her. She has been the one who has been the foundation of everything with her organising, visiting, and physical help. The Harborview doctor is Doctor Jones and we think he is the best.

They took a half dozen X-rays, gave us a lot of false hope that the Halo was coming off, then they changed their minds. There was no indication of anything wrong on the X-rays, but they were not sure everything had healed sufficiently. It is their policy to have seniors wear the Halo for four more weeks. It was tough not getting it off after looking forward to it so long, counting the days and nights.

Lilian left me on the 19th of November and I think she had given her all. She was wonderful. I admire her because it was something she had never done before. I was still in need of help in many ways, including having a companion to keep my spirits up as Lilian had done.

I was fortunate I had another friend who was willing to come and help me for a period. It was Wanda from Sarnia who came and gave me the help I needed. Wanda had to get familiar with all that it took to keep me going. She stayed about three weeks and was a great help. The thing that keeps me moving forward is the improvement I have had in my ability to move and the muscle control that I have gained. My life over the months that passed was devoted to increasing my mobility and muscles – working to become as independent as possible again.

It was to be a long, hard, uphill battle, but with optimism, help, and confidence, I struggled through the six months after the fall. Six grueling months of discomfort and soreness. Dr. Brown and his nurses from Everett Group Health supported me during this time, where they could, and by giving referrals to other doctors and facilities more familiar with spinal cord injury. I was progressing slowly. I am spending quite a lot of time on my computer writing a biography and sending emails.

My next goal was to find a used electric scooter. I go to Providence Hospital Rehab every Tuesday and Thursday. Not having any transport of my own, I have been using a volunteer transportation service called Catholic Chores. They have been wonderful and have helped me in every way possible. The gentleman who did most of the driving for me I can't say or thank him enough. My Acura Integra is very low and not suitable for conversion to an invalid vehicle.

Another challenge is taking driving lessons and finding a vehicle that is more suitable. I ended up with a Ford Econoline, equipped with a lift to raise my scooter into the cab. I had to have a hand control installed. It came with automatic opening doors and an electric seat that goes up and down and rotates to access the driver's seat. The driving control is for use with my left hand – back to accelerate and forward to brake.

Once all the controls were installed, my neighbor Ed and I went and picked it up and he drove us home. Once home he took me out in it for about an hour and from then on, I was on my own and everything has gone well since. I am perfectly comfortable driving it and except for a couple of mechanical failures of the lift and seat, I haven't had any trouble. I am told I have to have a test when my license needs to be renewed. That's when I will have the number plate changed for a handicap plate.

I am learning to live with my condition and accepting the fact that I may never walk again. This is a big change for me. I was water skiing on Lake Stevens four days before the accident. Dancing on the Cruise Lines, teaching x country skiing, and being able to do most things for myself.

It is quite a change in my life.

I plan on setting up my workshop to do cabinet making and any other woodwork project I can do. I used to oil paint and do photography and many other things, so I hope to pick that up again. I hope to meet people to share activities with. I find it very difficult to ask people to help me to do those things.

It is just over two years now since I had the accident, and a lot of things have happened. I tried sketching and water colours, but I have not been able to raise much enthusiasm to do much.

My Physical Therapy at Providence was with a lady called Peggy followed by Jennifer. It went well and I managed to walk 113 feet with a walker, but the therapy was discontinued and I had to go to Group Health to continue. The therapist there had a different idea and said, "Carry on your own".

I had been given a walker with four wheels and a seat, so when I walked to the kitchen, I could sit on it and move around, which I thought would be helpful, but it kept tipping back so trying to use it alone at home was too risky.

Due to a side effect from a medication, I got a bladder infection. I slowly lost my ability to walk the 113 feet and could only just about stand up. I told the doctor at the Capitol Hill Group Health and he gave me a referral for some more therapy at Group Health in Everett. The atmosphere and attitude of the people there was not like Providence, and the most I walked in the two months going once a week was 25 feet.

I am not giving up. I am going to try to get something made or do something that will help me with the walker. I have also start swimming to make my legs work better. I really wanted to walk. I requested another prescription of Baclofen hoping it would relieve the tightness around my knees that is stopping me from walking. My knees always feel as if there are straps around them stopping me from straightening.

The pills made me weak and tired. I backed off the medication and went to acupuncture for eight weeks. I had four sessions of massage and went for an interview with a chiropractor. He said the problem with my knees is nerve damage and could not be helped. I have overcome the bladder infections. Maurice my neighbour, and I worked on the four-wheel walker I got from Group Health this weekend and between the two of us we decided the back wheels could be reversed to help the tipping problem. It worked and the tipping problem is solved.

I have started swimming on Tuesday and Thursday evenings. I am going to try to make another effort to walk again – the third time. Throughout the whole period I have been home from the accident I have had many caring and helpful people. My neighbour and good friend Ed, has helped and supported me so much. He is always there giving me support. Jamie was coming and working in my workshop and getting my wood everyday through the last winter and I would have been lost without him. Carole has been emailing me every day, and coming over to help often. I had a lady named Virginia for a while, then she left and recommended another one named Karen who stayed for a long time. She was a thoughtful, nice and willing person. She moved too far away to get here for the few hours she worked. I have gotten another person to clean for me now. Alice is a good friend. She spent about six hours this weekend and thoroughly cleaned my toilets, floors and the rest of the house. It is now cleaner than it has been for a long time. I have known Alice for many years. A true friend.

I was a member of the Everett Elks, Eagles, Sons of Norway, and VFW, but have had no help from any of those organizations. The Seattle Mountaineers have been in contact with me and offered transportation to attend their functions. The Boeing Bluebirds have offered assistance and helped with my ramp and visited a few times bringing a handmade lap blanket and hat.

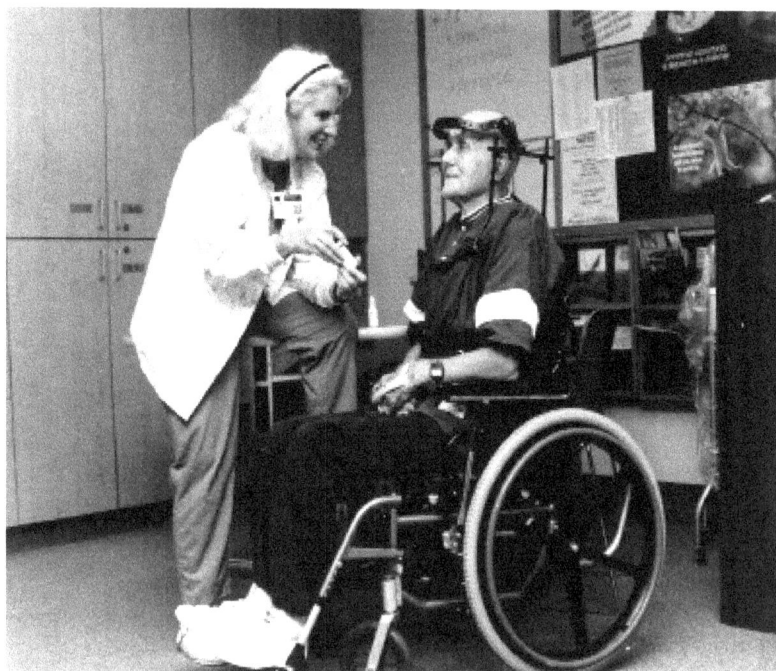

Hospital days in Everett, working hard to get home

Chapter 15

TREE ON HOUSE

Tree on Lake Stevens house

I was out for the evening at a family get together on Easter Day. After a pleasant evening, I arrived home with Cathy and Jamie who were transporting me. It was before I had my own transportation. The evening had been windy and we saw a few small branches on the road and we had to weave around a tree. There was a large branch at the beginning of the driveway. As we came up to the house, we saw a large tree had fallen across the roof. It was found out later to be a hemlock – 130 feet tall, and 2 feet in diameter. It crashed through the roof and ceiling.

It was three months since I had returned home from the hospital.

Just what I needed to speed my recovery.

The tree came to rest on the outer wall which was well constructed with 2"x 6", the latest code to allow for extra insulation. It stretched completely across the house and 30 ft over the other side where it snapped off. It smashed five trusses and the skylight in the bathroom. What a mess! Fortunately, it wasn't raining at the time and didn't damage the carpet and furniture.

Jamie went inside first, then came out and said it is too bad to go in. I wasn't feeling so bad that I couldn't handle another challenge in my life, so I had them get my wheelchair from the back of the car and take me in. When we came into the house, the beams were hanging halfway down to the floor all splintered. The plasterboard that hadn't fallen off was hanging halfway to the floor, and the insulation was piled up about two feet deep, so it was impossible to see across the room. Fortunately, it missed the chimney or the house could have burnt down.

When we first came in, Jamie and Cathy said, "You can't stay here. You will have to come and stay with us". I looked around and said this will clean up. "I am staying here."

I am organized in my own surroundings with all the things related to taking care of myself. I couldn't imagine how I would be in another house. I asked for a broom. I have one with a short handle and using that and my wheelchair as a snowplow, I pushed the insulation away to make a path. I then set to clearing up. We all chipped in and soon made a big impression on it.

I phoned Ed and he turned up with his son, so there were five grownups and two kids working on shoveling insulation into plastic bags and taking out wood and roofing. It wasn't too long before it was clear enough for me to move around in my wheelchair.

I stayed there alone that night. It was certainly a large tree to have to get off the roof. Again, Ed to the rescue. He has a large tractor with bucket and backhoe. The next morning, he came over and with the help of my youngest son Michael, they cut all the branches from the tree and cut the trunk into smaller pieces. Last was the largest and heaviest part of the trunk. They rolled it off the roof leaving a large hole. Fortunately, it was all cleared before the rain started – they covered the hole with plastic. Insurance was called and 2 days later there was someone here to estimate the damage. I phoned around to a few contractors and the insurance company's own contractor.

They all put in their estimates and after a week the insurance was settled. Fortunately, I was able to keep my bedroom warm enough but it was rough with the roof open and having to get up in the middle of the night to use the washroom with the temperature at 28 degrees. I had the wood fire and plenty of wood to try to keep the place warm during the day. Finally, the contractors came in and started working. I chose an old friend's son to do the work for me, Michael Olson. It took them about three weeks and except for the inconvenience of mess, dust and smell, everything went quite well. It's been a tough time but I am none the worse for it and have learnt a few things.

I had ten trees topped and two taken completely down to prevent another incident.

Chapter 16

TWO YEARS HAVE PASSED

My grandson Dylan, Mike and Mary's first born. Danielle's brother.

The fall now is history and I have got to review where am I and where am I going. I am living alone and independently. I have had a lot of work done inside and out of the house. I have an electric scooter and a Dodge van with hand controls. It is smaller and easier to drive.

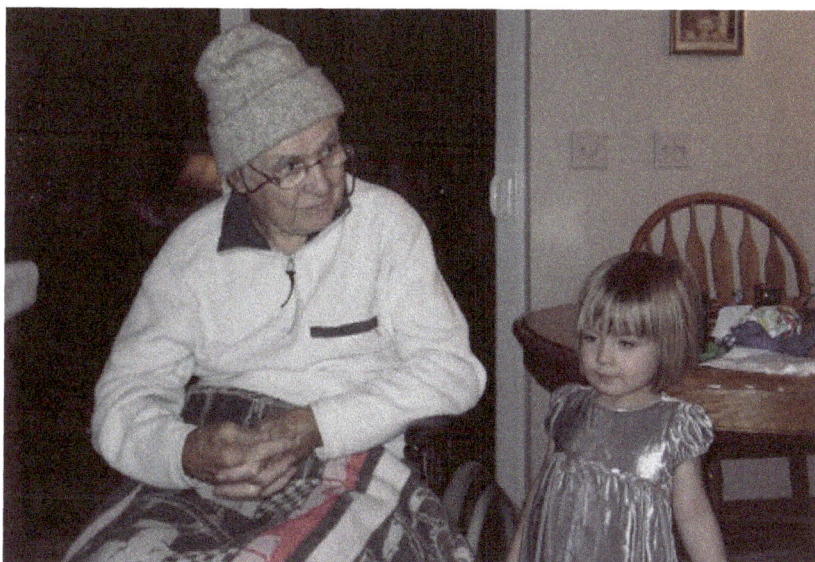

Second grandchild, Danielle and Dylan's sister.

Dad & Mary, ready to start their 60 day Asia & Pacific Explorer Cruise
September 27, 2002

EPILOGUE

This is where Bob, my dad, finished his Autobiography. With the help of memory and emails, Bob's eldest, his daughter Carole Scanes, will finish his last chapter.

With sadness, but also pride in the man that my father, Robert Edward Scanes was, I will summarize the last years of Dad's life in order to be able to share his Autobiography with family and others that might be interested.

Dad continued to live independently in his home in Lake Stevens on 5 acres by himself for several years. Using his Tool & Die skills, he built the tools to build a violin during the time he had at home.

Robert (usually known as Bob) was a very talented craftsmen having built furniture over the years. He would often watch Bob Ross and create some amazing paintings of which we all kept. I created a calendar from photos of his craftsmanship to share with family and friends after he passed away. He was a great soup maker, often making his own curry blends. Everything went into his soups!

Dad had many house guests during this time. Some wonderful friends that he had met on his many cruises. Dancing partners and wonderful ladies from many different areas. Certainly, Dad had great British charm, and the wonderful ability to communicate and keep in touch with friends.

It was while on a 60 day Asia & Pacific cruise in 2002 that Dad's independence vanished. It all started with a simple bladder infection that put him into a hospital in Gilroy, CA. Discouraging Dad from the lengthy cruise was fruitless. He was determined. He was traveling with his Norwegian friend Mary.

I flew down to bring Dad home where he went into Everett General hospital. He picked up a Staph infection, Mersa, that really took his energy away. Mersa was new and very contagious. It took a while to find a Care Center that would take him with Mersa. Skagit Valley Life Care Center in Sedro-Woolley finally did. After months of work, successes and failures, it became evident that Dad was very unlikely to move back into his house.

On September 10, 2006, Robert Edward Scanes passed away.

We held a Celebration of Life in Everett in October 2006. Scott, Mavis and I scattered Dad's ashes in the mountains where he spent many days skiing and hiking. I added his name to his mum and dad's tombstone in Addlestone, Surrey, England, scattering some ashes on the grave as well as into the canal that he bicycled by on his way to work when we lived there.

I miss my dad every day. He was such a strong and positive force and influence in my life. He instilled values that have made me and my brothers who we are today. We were fortunate to have loving, caring parents. Both did the best they could, leaving their families behind to find a better life for us.

Love and miss you Robert, Rob, Bob, Dad.

A FINAL WORD

September 30, 2006, Scott, Mavis, Tripper and I went over Snoqualmie Pass and hiked up to the Mountaineers Lodge. We scattered Dad's ashes. We drove up to Stampede Pass where Dad used to ski with the Mountaineers. We hiked to an area where Scott and I skied with Dad. It was a gorgeous day. The clouds disappeared right before we got there, and the sky was a deep blue. Many trees were brilliant with color. We scattered Dad's ashes into the wind. Some were very light and blew across the mountain and into the trees. The sun shone into them and they sparkled. The heavier pieces fell to the ground where all the colors of fall lay. Scarlet red vine maples and bright yellow bracken filled in with the vibrant green of young Doug Firs. It was emotional, both painful and healing. Scott packed Tripper (our kitten) in his backpack. Certainly, an unusual adventure for a cat. Dad had enjoyed her company several times over the summer, so it was fitting that we bring her. We saved some ashes to go back to England next trip to put with his mum and dad in the Addlestone Cemetery.

Robert Edward Scanes was an extraordinary man and he leaves behind many caring friends and family with many vivid memories of his desire to do his best at whatever he did. His unflagging determination was an inspiration to us all.

We miss you Dad!
Your loving daughter & sons,
Carole Roberta Scanes
Jamie Robert Scanes
Michael Robert Scanes

ACKNOWLEDGEMENTS

Robert Scanes started writing his autobiography after his accident in 1996. It has taken me, his daughter Carole, years to collect my emotions enough to verify, proof and prepare his book for publication. As this was my first experience with book publishing it was an enormous undertaking with many decisions to be made. Along the way I appreciated help from author, Peter Keim and friend and neighbour, Kevin Tighe. Peter helped with formatting, proofing and helpful advice. Kevin also helped with proofing and advice. Gratefulness also extends to Maddie Sweeney, a book designer who was recommended by Village Books. Maddie and I texted, emailed and met in person over many cups of coffee to keep moving forward. This would not be happening without Maddie's help! Chloe Hovind at Village Books in Fairhaven was also very involved in keeping the project moving forward. Her advice and diligence were outstanding. The publishing program at Village Books is thorough and worth the cost. Thank-you to my husband, Scott for listening and understanding during the years it took to complete this project. With heartfelt emotion, thanks to our dad for writing and sharing his interesting life. Lastly, thank-you to you the reader for reading Life of a Cockney.

Printed in the USA
CPSIA information can be obtained
at www.ICGtesting.com
JSHW071936211123
52187JS00010B/191

9 798218 170530